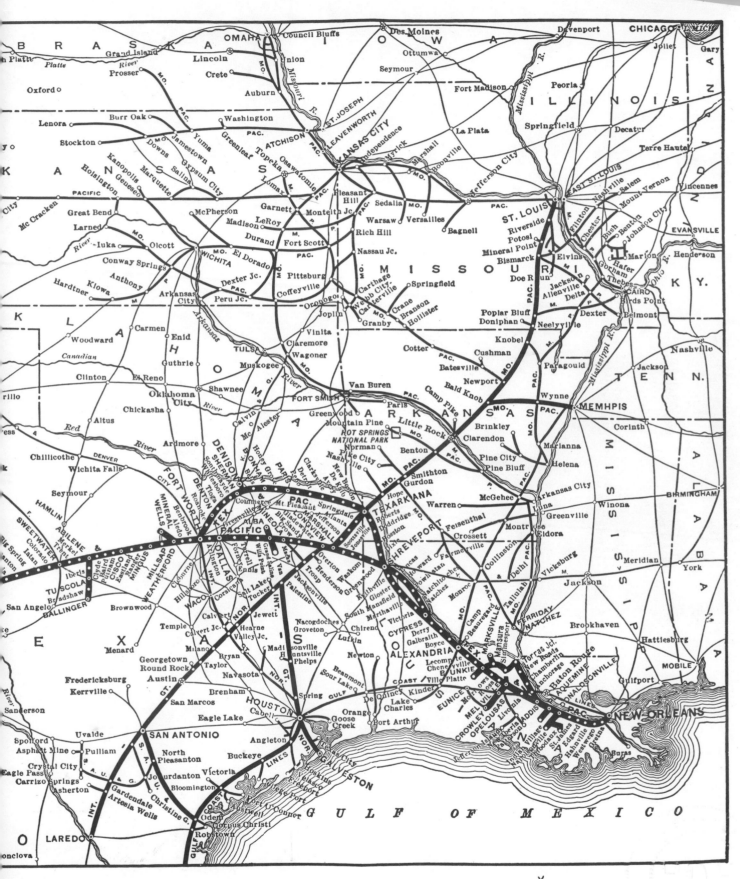

Janice &
KEN 10-90

Super-Power to Streamliners

THE
TEXAS & PACIFIC
RAILWAY

SUPER-POWER TO STREAMLINERS

1925-1975

JOE G. COLLIAS

M M BOOKS

CRESTWOOD,
MISSOURI

THE
TEXAS & PACIFIC
RAILWAY
SUPER-POWER TO STREAMLINERS
1925-1975

JOE G. COLLIAS

© Copyright 1989 by M M Books

Published and distributed by

M M BOOKS
CRESTWOOD, MISSOURI 63126 U.S.A.

Other books by Joe G. Collias

The Last of Steam

The Search For Steam

MoPac Power

Frisco Power

*Katy Power**

*(Co-authored by Raymond B. George)

Dust Jacket Painting

The Texas' side of the Texarkana station is a veritable kaleidoscope of color as Mountain type No. 900, in *Eagle* blue and gray, pulls smartly away from the station platforms with No. 7, *The Southerner,* while GP-7 No. 1113 idles nearby in Swamp Holly Orange and black.

-Painting by Joe G. Collias

Library of Congress Cataloging in Publication Data

Collias, Joe G.
    The Texas & Pacific Railway: super-power to streamliners, 1925-1975/Joe G. Collias.
    p. cm.
    Includes index.
    ISBN 0-9612366-2-0
    1. Locomotives—United States. 2. Texas & Pacific Railway.
I. Title.
TJ603.3.T4C65 1989
385'.0973—dc19   89-2675
                                                                                        CIP

Printed and bound in the United States of America

M M BOOKS
P.O. BOX 29318, CRESTWOOD, MISSOURI 63126

TABLE OF CONTENTS

ACKNOWLEDGMENTS

Following a perusal of this work it should be readily apparent that two individuals are responsible, in a large measure, for its photographic content. Regardless of its popularity, in Texas or elsewhere, the Texas and Pacific Railway had relatively few photographers frequenting its properties. In view of this relative pictorial scarcity, it is fortunate that each frequented a distinctly different portion of the railroad thus allowing for more diverse coverage. Aside from the more publicized railroad photographers, there were those who went their way in relative obscurity recording the railroad scene in their local area with enthusiasm and thoroughness. The latter was the case with the two principal contributors hereto: Roger S. Plummer, Sr., deceased, and Ed C. Robinson.

Born in Portland, Oregon, in 1899, Roger S. Plummer, Sr., came to Sulphur Springs, Texas, in 1936, to manage a newly built Carnation Company milk plant. He was an avid railfan and a prolific photographer of all rail activity in east Texas. Almost without exception, he set aside one day a week to use his Kodak Medalist II camera to record train movements. Even while acting in his official managerial position at the Carnation plant, he was apt to leave his office, board the motive power of the Cotton Belt local switching on the plant trackage, and, while the crew sat in the shade, perform the role of engineer. He loved to boast of his Presidency of the Carnation Belt, Sulphur Bluff and Pacific Railroad — the 1,000 feet of trackage within the plant area. Mr. Plummer was generous with his photographic material; supplying prints to anyone displaying a mutual interest. His work has been publicized frequently in various railroad periodicals and in other books by this author.

If Mr. Plummer, Sr., was east Texas' most prolific rail photographer then our second primary contributor could be termed the T&P's own photographer. Especially so in Louisiana. Ed C. Robinson, a native of Shreveport, Louisiana, began photographing the T&P in action in the late 1930's and continued to do so well after dieselization. He moved from track-side to cab-side, becoming a T&P fireman in 1945; leaving train service reluctantly to further his education and pursue a career in radio and later with the United States Post Office. Now retired, he is still an avid rail buff recalling vividly the days of steam and the engine crews with whom he worked.

As stated, the T&P had few photographers but all gave generously and enthusiastically to this work. It is doubtful if the enthusiasm displayed by Charles M. Mizell, Jr., of Dallas, Texas, or that of Tom Stamey of Fort Worth, Texas, for their favorite railroad, would vary one degree. Mr. Mizell possesses a personal, in-depth, knowledge of T&P steam power and is well-recognized for his authoritative articles on the subject in past issues of *Trains* Magazine. Mr. Stamey's interest in the T&P in general is evident in the authentically correct models of T&P equipment he creates and in his collection of all things T&P. Both of these T&P devotees gave generously of their time and material to enrich the pages following. Louis Saillard of Hammond, Louisiana, was helpful with needed information and photographs of the T&P, especially with regard to those engines disposed of to commercial interests.

No work of this nature would be complete without a generous showing of photographs from the steam locomotive negative collection of Charles T. Felstead of Chicago, Illinois. Provider to many an author, model importer, and periodical publisher, "Charlie" is always delighted to assist all who ask him for photos from his extensive, high quality collection. Once again, as in previous works of this author's, "Charlie's" collection is well represented.

Those who also assisted by furnishing much needed information and data were Charles A. Duckworth of Webster Groves, Missouri, David Sapp of Great Bend, Kansas, P. Allen Copeland of El Cajon, California, and Ray S. Curl of St. Louis, Missouri. Their enthusiastic response to the many questions posed by this author helped assure the accuracy of this work.

The author is grateful to all who assisted him. Photographic credits are shown wherever possible, where not, it may be correctly assumed the views are from the writer's acquired collection.

Photographer Ed Robinson enjoyed an unusual photographic perspective of the T&P — from the left side of the locomotive cab — during his tenure as fireman for the road. Memorable views of Ten-Wheelers Nos. 332 and 359 meeting with Louisiana division passenger runs near Shreveport, in 1942, were the result.

FOREWORD

Texas and Pacific! A title akin to the legendary Union Pacific itself! A name that elicits visions of transcontinental greatness with rails spanning the seemingly limitless width and breadth of Texas, reaching out across the desert expanse of the great southwest and on to the western edge of the American continent and the Pacific Ocean. What was to have become the southernmost transcontinental rail route in the United States got no farther than a junction with the usurper of its own intent, the Southern Pacific, at a barren point named Sierra Blanca, ninety-two miles east of El Paso, Texas. This, in itself, however, was no small accomplishment, since with inclusion of this mileage over the Southern Pacific into El Paso the Texas and Pacific Railway extended its rails a notable 1,167 miles — from the banks of the Mississippi River at New Orleans toward the desired objective — before reasoning prevailed and the race between the two railroads ceased. Slightly over 800 more miles of track would have been needed to reach the fabled gold coast.

This failure of the Texas and Pacific to meet its objective of the California coast is probably the most colorful in a history ripe with contests over building rights and although this writer by no means intends to retell the railroad's history, it is an appropriate and inclusive part. For a more comprehensive history of the building of the Texas and Pacific see the detailed chronological report in G. S. Reed's, *A History of Texas Railroads,* St. Clair Publishing Co., Houston, Texas, 1941, and the article entitled "Straight Through Texas," by David P. Morgan, *Trains* Magazine, March 1950.

The Texas Pacific Railroad (the "and" was inserted into its name in 1872) had, from the beginning, been planned to follow the magical 32nd parallel from Texas to the west coast and thus become the first transcontinental rail link to California. President Pierce, in 1854, went to the extent of paying Mexico ten million dollars for a portion of the land over which the line would pass. Enter 1861 and with it the bloody and bitter Civil War. Jefferson Davis' Confederacy did not need the route to California as much as it needed the iron rails of the T&P's predecessor roads for cannonballs. It wasn't until March 1871 that the Texas Pacific Railroad was formally chartered by Congress. No matter that by then the Union Pacific and Central Pacific had joined rails at Promontory, Utah, to become the first transcontinental system. San Diego, California, was still the dream of the TP's builders.

Unfortunately for the TP, one Collis P. Huntington — fresh from his success with the construction of the Central Pacific — had developed a strong opinion that railroads should be built from California east, not west toward the state. His now renamed Southern Pacific was already building eastward on the TP's original land grants along the 32nd parallel and well on its way to El Paso, Texas.

Under the able guidance of Jay Gould and General Grenville M. Dodge — the latter of Union Pacific construction fame — the Texas and Pacific track crews reached Sierra Blanca, Texas, 522 miles west of Fort Worth, Texas, where, on December 16, 1881, they met the eastward building track gangs of Huntington's Texas franchised Galveston, Harrisburg and San Antonio Railroad. Huntington's crews were intent on reaching San Antonio while Gould's T&P forces were set on a takeover — forceful if necessary — of trackage they considered their own by previous land grants. Violence would undoubtedly have occurred had Huntington and Gould not previously reached an agreement in the New York courts on November 26, 1881, settling their disputes over claims to land grants and rights of way in both New Mexico and Arizona. It was agreed that the T&P would relinquish all rights, title or interest in the SP's lines west of El Paso. In return it would be granted trackage rights for the 92 miles into El Paso for which it would pay half the cost of maintenance.

With completion of its own trackage into New Orleans, in 1882, the Texas and Pacific was essentially completed. It had become an important segment of a transcontinental route, and although it intersected the width of Louisiana it was essentially a Texas railroad and its destiny tied irrevocably to that of the state.

In reality — and in comparison with many first class railroads — the Texas and Pacific, with a sum total of 2,154 route miles, was a large railroad. Regardless of size and its Louisiana trackage, it was, without intent, a Texas' recluse. Texans have always admired "their" railroad and have shown a bitterness over the popularity of other more publicized rail systems. Fostered by Jay Gould's appropriation of T&P funds for the purchase of new rolling stock for his more favored Missouri Pacific — with obsolete and rundown MoPac equipment sent to the T&P in return — and the generally acknowledged viewpoint that the T&P had always been looked upon as a feeder by its parent Missouri Pacific Lines, admirers of the Texas and Pacific have felt both frustration and pride.

Although the Missouri Pacific indeed controlled the Texas and Pacific through a majority ownership of 74.7 percent of its stock, the Texas and Pacific objected vigorously to being called a Missouri Pacific subsidiary and long maintained its independent status. There was little denying the fact, though, that the Texas and Pacific's most strategic and lucrative traffic connection was with the Missouri Pacific at Texarkana, Texas. Since its inception, this transfer terminal with the St. Louis, Iron Mountain and Southern (later Missouri Pacific Lines) was the major artery for Texas and Pacific freight and passenger traffic.

Regardless of any such close ties, the Texas and Pacific motive power department went its own way, its locomotives having little resemblance to those of the Missouri Pacific. The advent of diesel power on the road brought with it a more visual indication of the parent road's control. The earliest of these locomotives displayed a final defiant note of independence in their coat of bright orange and black but the MoPac's own blue and gray soon covered all with only the corporate buzz saw and diamond emblems, aside from road names and engine numbers, denoting ownership.

The logical pattern in a merger is the inevitable phasing out of one corporate emblem or "logo" with the dominant company's emblem usually prevailing. Accordingly, in May 1963, the Texas and Pacific's diamond-shaped emblem was abandoned in favor of the MoPac buzz saw containing therein an all-too-temporary "Texas Pacific Lines." Full merger, only a matter of legal restraint, occurred on October 15, 1976.

The Texas and Pacific and the Missouri Pacific were completely dieselized by the date of the merger; the T&P's last steam locomotive, 2-10-4 No. 650, having been retired and scrapped in 1953. While steam was the dominant power on both carriers its appearance was a marked extreme; the MoPac never varying from the "only color for a steam locomotive is black" philosophy advocated by its one-time President Lewis W. Baldwin. T&P management, on the other hand, admired a bit of flash in the way of gray-green boiler and cylinder jacketing, nickel-plated cylinder heads and stack flanges, and bold, gold lettering and numbers. Such coloration was not confined to passenger power alone as it was freely applied to freight and switching power alike. The advent of the blue and gray painted diesel power for the new *Texas Eagle,* in 1948, saw a number of Pacific and Mountain type steam locomotives repainted to match. Suffice it to say, although the MoPac originated the *Eagle* color scheme and operated a veritable fleet of the *Eagle* streamliners, not one MoPac steamer was ever painted to match.

The T&P's roster of steam motive power was not always so colorful or varied. Before World War I the carrier rolled its freight and passenger trains alike behind a roster of 4-6-0 Ten-Wheelers and 2-8-0 Consolidation types. Classically simple in design they were capable of wheeling a respectable size train across the undulating Texas' topography. The years immediately following World War I would bring dramatic changes to this simplistic roster. The year 1916 brought both bankruptcy and one John Lynch Lancaster — one of two court appointed receivers for the road — along with the first 2-10-2 wheel arrangements. History would shortly record which was the more important occurrence for the T&P. In 1919, the United States Railroad Administration assigned two more new wheel arrangements to the road in the form of government designed 0-6-0 switchers and light 2-8-2 Mikado types. The same year would also witness the first of an eventual twenty-two 700 class 4-6-2 Pacific types powering the lengthier and heavier steel passenger car consists. Altogether a momentous period in the forming of the T&P's steam locomotive roster and yet relatively obscured by the changes yet to come under Mr. Lancaster's able leadership.

While these early motive power acquisitions of the Lancaster administration were marked improvements to the T&P's steam roster the most notable additions occurred between 1925 and 1928. The former year mentioned witnessed the introduction of Lima Locomotive Co.'s "Super-Power" concept of the steam locomotive in the form of a 2-8-4 demonstrator called the A-1. Eventually this engine became the Illinois Central's No. 7049, and later its No. 8049. The engine was built to extoll the Lima principle of a generous boiler capacity, large grate areas over an articulated four-wheel trailing truck, lower combustion rates, superheated steam for all auxiliaries and a limited compensated cutoff in combination with the trailing truck booster. T&P officials, including John Lancaster, were evidently impressed with the A-1's performance but obviously felt the need for a slightly larger and more powerful machine. Basically a lengthened A-1 or 2-10-4 type was the result and ten such locomotives were ordered in July 1925. Except for an experiment with a 2-10-2 type on the Santa Fe, they were the first such wheel arrangement and were thus accorded the name Texas types in honor of their owner. These new machines were so impressive that by 1928 seventy of them were at work on the T&P. It is a generally accepted fact that the arrival of the I class 2-10-4's was the greatest single physical improvement ever effected by the T&P. It was certainly one of Mr. Lancaster's greatest achievements.

Overshadowed by the arrival of the new Super-Power — but just as notable in appearance and need — was the purchase of ten M-1 and M-2 class 4-8-2 Mountain types, in 1925 and 1928 respectively, that were sorely needed to power the ever increasing train lengths of the *Sunshine Special* coming off the rails of the Missouri Pacific at Texarkana, Texas. Even though of classic lines and modest dimensions, they were impressive additions to the roster. The first five engines of this group, Nos. 900-904, were rendered all the more imposing by the manner in which the Elesco feedwater heater was mounted completely forward of and high on the smokebox front. Accenting this effect was the placement of a tastefully colored red and blue cast metal Texas and Pacific emblem in front of the heater unit. Shielded air pumps on pilot beam, nickel-plated cylinder heads, stack flange and colored T&P emblems again displayed on the pump shields soon made these engines the ultimate in T&P motive power grandeur.

Freight classification yards received their share of needed new power at the same time. Fifteen 0-8-0 switchers that were basically copies of the USRA design were delivered by the Baldwin Locomotive Works, between 1925 and 1927, to sort all the added tonnage those new 2-10-4's were expected to bring. Four of these were built with tender truck mounted Franklin auxiliary locomotive boosters for hump yard work and as pushers on Baird Hill in far west Texas. The end of the 1920's saw the T&P with a steam roster second to none in the State of Texas and the southwest.

The beauty of T&P steam power is exemplified by No. 717 at Fort Worth, Texas, in 1940.

The way it was in a T&P loco-motive cab. Engineer Al Smith, a veteran in T&P en-gine service, strikes the arche-type pose as he opens the throttle of Pacific No. 701 to move train No. 27 away from the Shreveport station, in 1940. — *E. Robinson*

A bright, shiny face — crowned with flowing black oil smoke exhaust — speaks well for all of the T&P's meticulously maintained 4-6-0 Ten-Wheelers in passenger service. D-11-s No. 414 hurries west across a wintry Louisiana landscape, with train No. 27, on the run from Alexandria, Louisiana, to Marshall, Texas, in December 1947. — *E. Robinson*

EARLY POWER
...A Ten-Wheeler Monopoly

There is little in Texas that could be classed as conservative. To say the T&P's early steam roster was conservative might well raise the eyebrows of a true Texan. But conservative it was at the turn of the century. The 4-4-0 Eight-Wheelers of the road's infant years had almost totally been replaced with the 4-6-0 Ten-Wheeler type locomotive. This versatile, early dual-service engine monopolized the T&P roster from 1900 until the first of the ten F-1 class 2-8-0's arrived in 1912 with ten new class D-11 4-6-0's!

The Ten-Wheeler was an ideal locomotive for the roller coaster topography of the T&P. With the exception of big, bad, Baird Hill in west Texas, tonnage restrictive grades were almost nonexistent, the right-of-way adhering close to the undulating Texas' landscape. The husky Ten-Wheelers could haul an amazing amount of tonnage over such terrain, be it freight or passenger. A ten-to-twelve-car consist of the *Sunshine Special* behind a D-class Ten-Wheeler — albeit a nonair-conditioned consist — was not unusual. The wheel arrangement fared even better on the pool table topography of Louisiana.

Ten F-1 class 2-8-0 Consolidation types were purchased from the Baldwin Locomotive Works, in 1912, but, in contrast to other class one carriers that reordered the type in quantity, T&P chose not to increase this token amount. Texas' topography, again, was the reason. Built with 57-inch drivers for use in lugging freight up the 1.3 percent grade of Baird Hill, they were obviously too low-drivered to accelerate rapidly enough on downgrades to make it to the top of undulating grades elsewhere on the system.

Just as the 4-6-0 monopolized the main line, the 0-6-0 wheel arrangement monopolized the freight yards until the relatively late arrival of the 0-8-0 type in 1925. Remnants of the B-4 and B-5 class 0-6-0's frequented the yards of the T&P until their general retirement following World War I. Replacements arrived in the form of heavier and more powerful government designed USRA 0-6-0's, in 1919 and 1923. A large number of these B-8 class engines were still in active service in 1950.

A considerable number of the D-9 and D-10 class Ten-Wheelers were also still in active service in 1949-50 — downgraded to schedules less demanding but still giving a good account of themselves as the following photographs taken by Ed Robinson show.

T&P EARLY STEAM POWER IN SERVICE AFTER 1925

P — Passenger service
S — Freight service

Class and Service	Wheel Type	Numbers	Builder and Date	Cylinders (Bore x Stroke) (In Inches)	Drive Wheel Diameter (In Inches)	Boiler Pressure Lbs.	Grate Area (Sq. Ft.)	Engine Weight (Lbs.)	Tractive Force (Lbs.)	Remarks
A-3 P	4-4-0	16, 20	T&P 1900	17 x 24	63	150	15.5	81,000	14,000	Scrpd 1-29
A-3 P	4-4-0	109	Schen 1881	17 x 24	63	150	15.5	81,000	14,000	Scrpd 1-26
A-3 P	4-4-0	125	Pitts 1882	17 x 24	63	150	15.5	81,000	14,000	Scrpd 1-26
A-4 P	4-4-0	186	Rome 1887	18 x 24	63	150	18	95,000	15,700	Scrpd 1-26
C-1 S	2-6-0	147, 151, 153	Rogers 1883	19 x 22	52	145	22.7	88,000	19,200	Sold 1-26
D-2 F	4-6-0	82	Pitts 1881	17 x 24	57	145	15.5	91,000	15,000	Sold 1-25
D-3 F	4-6-0	163	Brooks 1886	18 x 24	57	150	17	94,000	19,400	See note

(Sold to Jefferson & North Western for their No. 163, 1-25)

Class and Service	Wheel Type	Numbers	Builder and Date	Cylinders (Bore x Stroke) (In Inches)	Drive Wheel Diameter (In Inches)	Boiler Pressure Lbs.	Grate Area (Sq. Ft.)	Engine Weight (Lbs.)	Tractive Force (Lbs.)	Remarks
D-3 F	4-6-0	165	Brooks 1886	18 x 24	52	150	17	94,000	17,400	Sold 1-25
D-4 F	4-6-0	171, 173, 181	Brooks 1886-87	18 x 24	57	150	16.75	97,000	17,400	Scrpd 1-26
D-4 F	4-6-0	174, 175	Rome 1887	18 x 24	52	150	16.75	97,000	19,400	Scrpd 1-26
D-4 F	4-6-0	180	Rome 1887	18 x 24	52	165	16.75	97,000	21,000	Sold 1-26
D-5 F	4-6-0	189-223	BLW 1889-90	19 x 24	57	150	17	121,000	19,400	See notes

(Originally built with 50 inch drive wheels and 21,500 Lb. TF. Rebuilt with 57 inch in 1899-90)
(Nos. 189, 194, 198, 199, 221 scrapped 1-26. All other Nos. scrapped 1927-48 or sold as listed below;

No. 191 to Gifford-Hill & Co., Inc., 1-46
No. 200 to Cinclair Central Factory
No. 203 to Eastland, Wichita Falls & Gulf Ry.
No. 204 to Gifford-Hill & Co., Inc.
No. 209 to Gifford-Hill & Co., Inc., 1-46
No. 217 to Gifford-Hill & Co., Inc., 1-46, thence to Evangeline Ry.
No. 220 to Gifford-Hill & Co., Inc., 3-48
No. 223 to Pecos Valley Ry., 5-47.

Class and Service	Wheel Type	Numbers	Builder and Date	Cylinders (Bore x Stroke) (In Inches)	Drive Wheel Diameter (In Inches)	Boiler Pressure Lbs.	Grate Area (Sq. Ft.)	Engine Weight (Lbs.)	Tractive Force (Lbs.)	Remarks
D-5 F	4-6-0	230-232	BLW 1893	19 x 24	57	150	17	121,000	19,400	See notes

(No. 230 sold to Gifford-Hill & Co., Inc. No. 231 to Rock Island Southern. No. 232 Scrapped 11-32)

| D-5 F | 4-6-0 | 233-238 | BLW 1897 | 19 x 24 | 57 | 175 | 17 | 121,000 | 22,600 | See notes |

(All on roster of 6-45. No. 235 sold to Central Texas Ry., Nos. 236 & 238 sold to Gifford-Hill & Co., Inc., 5-46)

| D-6 P | 4-6-0 | 224-229 | BLW 1892 | 19 x 24 | 63 | 165 | 31 | 131,500 | 19,300 | See note |

(All scrapped prior to 1925 except Nos. 224 and 225 scrapped 1-26)

D-7 P	4-6-0	239-244	BLW 1897	19 x 26	67	190	31	153,000	22,600	See note
D-7 P	4-6-0	264-266	Rogers 1900	19 x 26	67	190	31	153,000	22,600	See note
D-7 P	4-6-0	267-274	Cooke 1901	19 x 26	67	190	31	153,000	22,600	See note

(All D-7 class engines scrapped by 1-33)

| D-8 P | 4-6-0 | 245-256 | Rogers 1899 | 19 x 24 | 63 | 190 | 23 | 125,000 | 22,200 | See note |

(No. 248 sold to Saginaw & Manistee Ry. 2-43, No. 253 sold 1947, all others scrapped between 1926-1943)

Class and Service	Wheel Type	Numbers	Builder and Date	Cylinders (Bore x Stroke) (In Inches)	Drive Wheel Diameter (In Inches)	Boiler Pressure Lbs.	Grate Area (Sq. Ft.)	Engine Weight (Lbs.)	Tractive Force (Lbs.)	Remarks
D-9 F	4-6-0	257-263	Rogers 1900	20 x 26	63	200	36	158,000	28,000	Scrpd 1-26
D-9 F	4-6-0	275-291	Cooke 1901	20 x 26	63	200	36	158,000	28,000	See notes

(Nos. 275-277, 282 converted to D-9½ in 1907. No. 283 sold to International Creosote, then to Arkansas & Louisiana Missouri Ry. No. 285, 287 sold to U.S. Army, Camp Polk, La., 1941-42. No. 288 sold to Gifford-Hill & Co., Inc., 1946. All other numbers scrapped by 1947.)

Class and Service	Wheel Type	Numbers	Builder and Date	Cylinders	Drive Wheel Diameter	Boiler Pressure	Grate Area	Engine Weight	Tractive Force	Remarks
D-9 F	4-6-0	292-316	Cooke 1902	20 x 26	63	200	36	158,000	28,000	See notes

(No. 312 converted to D-9½ in 1907. All others scrapped by 1949 or sold as listed below;
No. 298 to Export-Import Co., 1-46
No. 305 to Paris & Mt. Pleasant R.R., 8-37
No. 301 to U.S. Army, Camp Claiborne, Tex., 5-42
No. 310 to U.S. Army, Camp Polk, La., 4-42
No. 302 to Paris & Mt. Pleasant R.R., 8-37
No. 314 to U.S. Army, Camp Polk, La., 4-42
No. 303 to Gifford-Hill & Co., Inc.
No. 316 to Paris & Mt. Pleasant R.R., 9-49)

Class and Service	Wheel Type	Numbers	Builder and Date	Cylinders	Drive Wheel Diameter	Boiler Pressure	Grate Area	Engine Weight	Tractive Force	Remarks
D-9 F	4-6-0	324-338	Cooke 1903	20 x 26	63	200	36	158,000	28,000	See note

(Nos. 326, 332, 334 converted to D-9½-s in 1907. No. 327 sold to Paris & Mt. Pleasant R.R., 11-36.
No. 333 to U.S. Army, Camp Polk, La., 3-42. All others scrapped by 1949)

Class and Service	Wheel Type	Numbers	Builder and Date	Cylinders	Drive Wheel Diameter	Boiler Pressure	Grate Area	Engine Weight	Tractive Force	Remarks
D-9 F	4-6-0	349-358	Rogers 1906	20 x 26	63	200	36	158,000	28,000	See note

(No. 358 converted to D-9½-s in 1910. No. 354 sold to Paris & Mt. Pleasant R.R., 8-37.
No. 357 sold to U.S. Army, Camp Polk, La., 3-42. All others scrapped by 1949)

Class and Service	Wheel Type	Numbers	Builder and Date	Cylinders	Drive Wheel Diameter	Boiler Pressure	Grate Area	Engine Weight	Tractive Force	Remarks
D-9½-s P	4-6-0	359-360	T&P 1907	20 x 26	67	200	36	162,000	26,373	
D-9½-s P	4-6-0	Below	T&P 1907-10	20 x 26	67	200	36	162,000	26,373	See notes

(Nos. 275-277, 282, 312, 326, 332, 334, 358 converted from D-9 class by T&P. All scrapped by 1950)

Class and Service	Wheel Type	Numbers	Builder and Date	Cylinders	Drive Wheel Diameter	Boiler Pressure	Grate Area	Engine Weight	Tractive Force	Remarks
D-10-s F	4-6-0	361-400	Cooke 1907	24 x 28	63	185	48.25	211,660	40,256	See notes

(Nos. 382, 390, 392, 395 equipped with Elesco K-31 Feedwater Heater.
Nos. 385, 396, 397, 399 equipped with Elesco K-30 Feedwater Heater.
No. 394 equipped with Worthington Feedwater Heater and pump.
Nos. 362, 381, 382, 387, 388, 390, 392, 393-397, 399 equipped with G-1 2-10-2 tenders.
Nos. 370-372, 374, 375, 377, 379 equipped with G-1-a 2-10-2 tenders.
Nos. 367, 376, 383, 386, 389, 391, 398, 400 equipped with G-1-b 2-10-2 tenders.
Nos. 366 and 369 equipped with P-1 4-6-2 tenders.
Nos. 380 and 394 equipped with P-1-r 4-6-2 tenders.
All numbers scrapped between 1945 and 1950.)

Class and Service	Wheel Type	Numbers	Builder and Date	Cylinders	Drive Wheel Diameter	Boiler Pressure	Grate Area	Engine Weight	Tractive Force	Remarks
D-11-s P	4-6-0	411-420	BLW 1912	21 x 28	67	200	35	196,800	31,300	Scrpd 11-49
E-1-s P	4-4-2	339, 340	T&P 1906	22 x 28	75	185	45	213,986	28,414	Scrpd 12-48
F-1 F	2-8-0	401-410	BLW 1912	24 x 30	57	180	49.5	210,800	46,383	Scrpd 12-48

(Nos. 401, 407 and 410 sold to Gifford-Hill & Co., Inc. in 1948. No. 407 to Evangeline Railway)

REV. J. 5-12-47 REVISED TO DATE. A.J.S. REV. K 9-17-49 ENG. 384 CANCELED. P.W.R. REV. L 11-14-49 ENG. NO. 385 REMOVED. A.J.S.

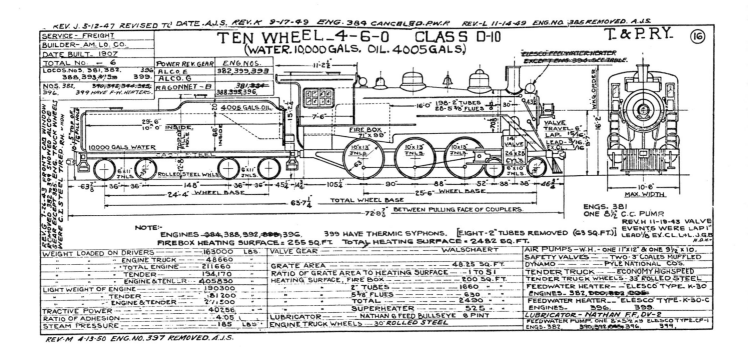

TEN WHEEL — 4-6-0 — CLASS D-10 — T. & P. RY. ⑯
(WATER. 10,000 GALS. OIL. 4005 GALS.)

REV. M 4-13-50 ENG. NO. 397 REMOVED. A.J.S.

REV. I 3-4-47 REVISED TO DATE. R.H. REV. J-5-12-47 REVISED TO DATE. A.J.S. REV. K 12-12-47 ENG. 416 ADDED. D.O.G.

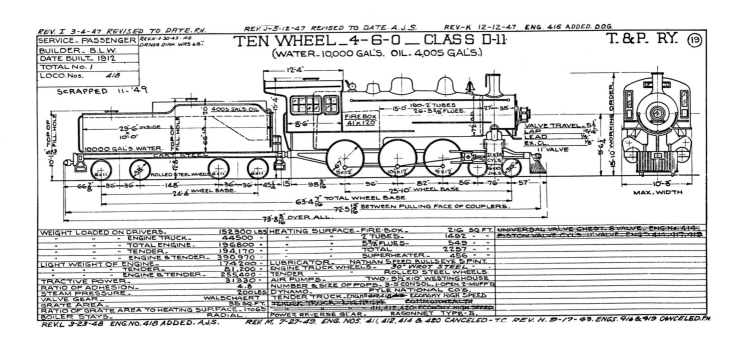

TEN WHEEL — 4-6-0 — CLASS D-11 — T. & P. RY. ⑲
(WATER. 10,000 GAL'S. OIL. 4,005 GAL'S.)

REV. L 3-23-48 ENG. NO. 418 ADDED. A.J.S. REV. M, 7-27-49, ENG. NOS. 411, 412, 414 & 420 CANCELED - T.C. REV. N. 9-17-49. ENGS. 416 & 419 CANCELED. P.W.

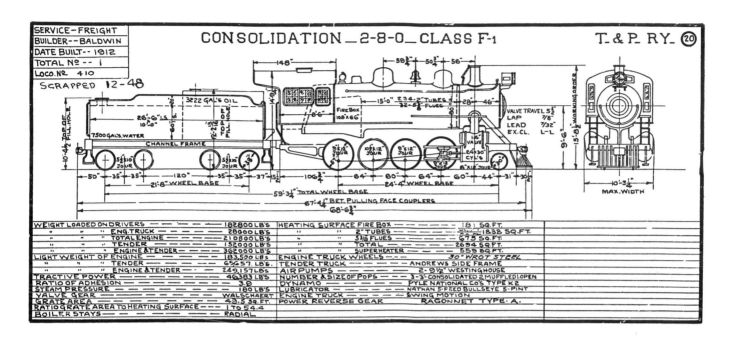

CONSOLIDATION _ 2-8-0 _ CLASS F-1   T.& P. RY. ⑳

WEIGHT LOADED ON DRIVERS — — — —	182800 LB'S	HEATING SURFACE FIRE BOX — — — — —	181 SQ.FT.
" " " ENG. TRUCK — — —	28000 LB'S	" " 2" TUBES — — — — —	1838 SQ.FT.
" " " TOTAL ENGINE — — —	210800 LB'S	" " 5⅛ FLUES — — — — —	675 SQ.FT.
" " " TENDER — — — —	152000 LB'S	" " TOTAL — — — —	2694 SQ.FT.
" " " ENGINE & TENDER — — —	362000 LB'S	" " SUPERHEATER — — — —	559 SQ.FT.
LIGHT WEIGHT OF ENGINE — — — —	183,500 LB'S	ENGINE TRUCK WHEELS —. — —	30" WROT STEEL
" " TENDER — — — —	65657 LB'S.	TENDER TRUCK — — —	ANDREWS SIDE FRAME
" " ENGINE & TENDER — — —	249,157 LB'S	AIR PUMPS — — — —	2-9½" WESTINGHOUSE
TRACTIVE POWER — — — — — —	46383 LB'S	NUMBER & SIZE OF POPS — — —	3-3" CONSOLIDATED 2 MUFFLED 1 OPEN
RATIO OF ADHESION — — — — —	3.9	DYNAMO — — — —	PYLE NATIONAL CO'S TYPE K2
STEAM PRESSURE — — — — —	180 LB'S	LUBRICATOR — — — —	NATHAN 5-FEED BULLSEYE 5-PINT
VALVE GEAR — — — — —	WALSCHAERT	ENGINE TRUCK — — — —	SWING MOTION
GRATE AREA — — — —	49.5 SQ.FT.	POWER REVERSE GEAR	RAGONNET TYPE A.
RATIO GRATE AREA TO HEATING SURFACE — — —	1 TO 54.4		
BOILER STAYS — — — — —	RADIAL		

Indicative of several antiquated, but active, locomotives on the T&P's roster, in 1925, was 4-4-0 American type No. 125 — an 1882 product of Pittsburgh Locomotive Works. The engine was one of six similar 4-4-0's still in steam that were disposed of when new 2-10-4 and 4-8-2 types arrived. — *Ray S. Curl Collection*

Notwithstanding its relatively low 63-inch drivers, D-8 No. 248 is a fine example of T&P's turn-of-the-century Ten-Wheelers that powered its secondary passenger trains until the late 1920's. A product of Rogers Locomotive Works in 1898, it strikes a classic pose awaiting departure from the Paris, Texas, station en route to Fort Worth with train No. 31 in February 1927. — *Railroad Museum of Pennsylvania (PHMC)*

Tall-stacked and as prim and pretty as a Ten-Wheeler could be, T&P No. 312, a class D-9½-s, sits at the Denton, Texas, station on June 30, 1938, at the head-end of train No. 32 on the Fort Worth to Texarkana line. No. 312 was one of eleven original class D-9 Ten-Wheelers randomly selected and converted to D-9½-s — between 1907 and 1910 — with new carbon steel frames, Walschaert valve gear, 67-inch drivers, and super-heated. The D-10 classification had already been assigned to the forty locomotives, Nos. 361-400, built in 1907, hence the ½ fraction designation. — *C. M. Mizell, Jr.*

Local freight on the T&P, in 1943, meant any one of a number of 4-6-0's on the head-end. D-9½-s Ten-Wheeler No. 276 waits at the Bunkie, Louisiana, depot platform while its crew receives switching instructions from the agent. — *E. Robinson*

Although designated as a freight engine for most of its 50 years of existence, D-9 4-6-0 No. 331 still displays a gray-green boiler jacket, cylinders and sand and steam domes in this late-in-life portrait at Addis, Louisiana, in November 1951. — *C.T. Felstead Collection*

What at first glance appears to have been the most direct and heavily traveled route between Shreveport, Louisiana, and Texarkana, Texas, was, instead, a lightly ballasted line with scheduled mixed train service only, each way, every other day except Sunday. For more efficient connections — west or north — all main line traffic went via the original T&P line to Marshall, Texas. Listed in the timetables as the TS&N (Texarkana, Shreveport and Natchez Railway Company) branch, the lines 55-pound rail seldom carried anything heavier than the likes of D-9 Ten-Wheeler No. 330 shown here rolling south near Belcher, Louisiana, with an auxiliary water car, four cars of pulpwood logs, seven miscellaneous freight cars, and a combination caboose-coach, on February 22, 1939. — *A. E. Brown, dec., L. Saillard Collection*

That the T&P's route across the State of Louisiana was gradeless enough to allow locomotives of relatively small size to wheel considerable size consists with ease is well-evidenced in this view of D-9½-s Ten-Wheeler No. 359 about to cross the Louisiana, Arkansas & Texas main line near Greenwood, Louisiana, in June 1941, with eight heavyweight cars of train No. 27 on the Alexandria, Louisiana, to Marshall, Texas, run. — *E. Robinson*

Two of the D-9½-s class Ten-Wheelers at Shreveport, Louisiana, in 1949. No. 326 sports a gray-green boiler and cylinder jacket while No. 359 is in all black attire. — *No. 326, H. K. Vollrath; No. 359, R. Collins*

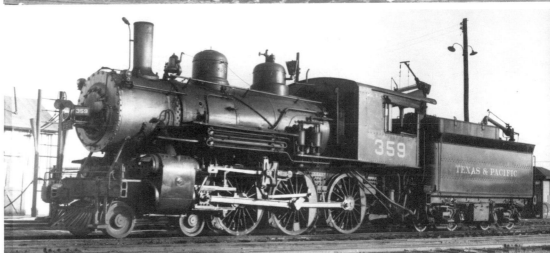

Below: Photographed by Ed Robinson from a moving automobile on the paralleling highway, D-9½-s Ten-Wheeler No. 332 is rolling along at close to fifty miles an hour near Lake Hayes, Louisiana, on a fall day in 1941, with train No. 20. Watching the rod and valve motion of a steamer for mile after mile from this viewpoint bordered on the hypnotic.

Relatively low 63-inch drivers on D-10-s Ten-Wheeler No. 383 are apt evidence of its intended use as heavy freight power when purchased from American Locomotive in October 1907. Its assignment is the same in this 1947 view as it waits to forward an extra freight west from the Fort Worth, Texas, yards. — *C. T. Felstead*

Largest and last of the Ten-Wheeler types on the T&P, D-11-s No. 416 sports nickel-plated cylinder head covers and spoked pilot truck wheels in this 1947 view. Baldwin built ten of these as class D-11, in June 1912, at a time when they were considered the last word in heavy passenger power. — *C. T. Felstead*

Referred to locally as "the bullet," the local freight from Texarkana, Texas, rolls into Shreveport, Louisiana, behind 4-6-0 No. 352, with more show than speed. An auxiliary water car is coupled behind the engine's tender to help speed the schedule. — *E. Robinson*

The Japanese attack on Pearl Harbor is as yet unsuspected but imminently near as D-10-s 4-6-0 No. 392 hurries a military extra west through Bunkie, Louisiana, in September 1941. The head brakeman stands ready to snare train orders on the fly. — *E. Robinson*

Its high-mounted Elesco feed-water heater and off-center headlight imparting an appearance akin to that of a Canadian National freight hog, D-10-s Ten-Wheeler No. 385 waits for a clear signal at Denton, Texas, in May 1948. The D-10-s, along with ten 2-8-0 types, were the largest power on the T&P until the first 2-10-2's arrived in 1916. The application of Elesco heaters to eight of the class created a distinctive, and rare appearance seen on few Ten-Wheeler types. No. 388 of the class was the last steam locomotive in service on the T&P, ending all steam operations with a Shreveport to Alexandria local on February 20, 1952. — C. M. Mizell, Jr.

Branch line chores were a common assignment for Ten-Wheelers, in the later years of steam, but No. 399, with its Elesco feedwater heater atop its smokebox, is a rather impressive looking engine for the job of wheeling a local freight over the ten-mile branch between Grand Saline and Alba, Texas, in June 1949. — R. S. Plummer, Sr., dec.

It is the winter of 1942 and the United States of America and its Allies are engaged in a mighty struggle to survive. Midway in train No. 27, running from Alexandria, Louisiana, to Marshall, Texas, behind 4-6-0 No. 419, is one of the T&P's more colorful forms of support — a red, white, and blue painted coach urging all who saw it to "Buy War Bonds." — *E. Robinson*

Venting an outpouring of smoke exhaust more indicative of a Union Pacific Challenger type cresting Sherman Hill in far-off Wyoming, Ten-Wheeler No. 416 blackens the bayous west of Shreveport, Louisiana, while hurrying train No. 27 toward Marshall, Texas. — *E. Robinson*

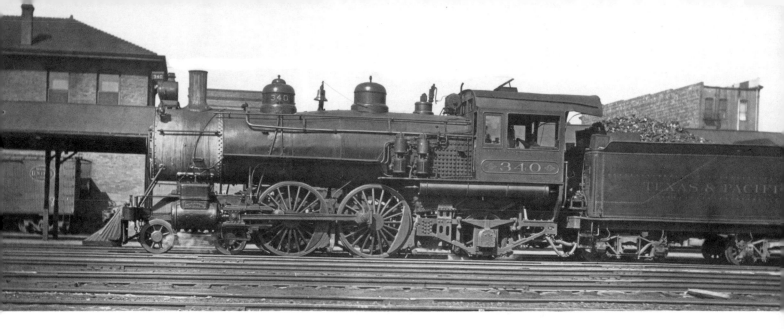

A rare photograph of No. 340 of the ill-fated class E-1-s Atlantic types, Nos. 339-340, shows the engine in service at Texarkana, Texas, in 1920, in its as-built condition. Its most apparent difference is the use of a fixed-frame Hodge type trailing truck as opposed to the later applied swivel-mounted Delta truck. Early use of the company emblem in locomotive decoration is evident in the two diamond shapes enclosed within the raised scrollwork on the cab side. — *Railroad Museum of Pennsylvania (PHMC)*

A second and almost identically posed company photograph of No. 340 taken after its first shopping reveals a change in the cab side and of the trailing truck. Built at the T&P's own Marshall, Texas, shops in 1906 and intended for improving passenger train schedules across the Texas' plains, its tractive effort of 28,414 pounds was far inferior to that of the best of T&P's 4-6-0's. With its headlamp mounted atop the smokebox and trailing a tender reminiscent of a Civil War era 4-4-0, the engine hardly evoked the look of the high-wheeled speedster normally associated with the wheel arrangement. No further Atlantic types were built by the T&P.

Super-Power wasn't always needed to produce a voluminous cloud of smoke and steam. Ten-Wheeler No. 415, a D-11-s, smokes up the Anna Street overpass in Shreveport, Louisiana, heading for Alexandria with passenger run No. 20. — *E. Robinson*

In common with all Gould-owned carriers at the turn of the century, the T&P's roadbed was so poor that locomotives with four-wheel lead trucks and better tracking ability were preferred over those with two-wheel trucks. Aside from twenty earlier built 2-6-0's assigned to yard service, the only two-wheel lead truck locomotives ordered before the class G 2-10-2's in 1916, were ten class F-1 2-8-0's, Nos. 401-410, purchased from Baldwin in 1912. Although a favorite of many rail carriers, such was not the case with the T&P as duplicates were not ordered. They served as yard switchers and local power, until all were either scrapped or sold by December 1948.

One exception to the T&P's scrapping of the F-1 class was No. 407, sold to Gifford-Hill & Company, Inc., in 1948, for hauling gravel on the firm's own Evangeline Railway, where it remained in active service until 1953. Appearing polished and well-maintained, No. 407 sits for its portrait at Evangeline Junction, Louisiana, in November 1952. — *A. E. Brown, dec., L. Saillard Collection*

His arm outstretched in a manner of greeting commonplace in steam's glory days, T&P's engineer Walter Simpson has Ten-Wheeler No. 416 charging across the bayou bottoms near Lake Hayes, Louisiana, at a mile-a-minute with the seven cars of No. 20, a Marshall, Texas, to Alexandria, Louisiana, passenger haul. — *E. Robinson*

The Gifford-Hill & Company, Inc. — a construction firm with operations in Texas and Louisiana — was one of the largest buyers of obsolete T&P steam motive power. Starting with D-4 Ten-Wheeler No. 175 in December 1928, and ending with B-6 0-6-0 No. 320 in 1951, the firm purchased a total of 25 small locomotives rendered obsolete by the larger and more modern power bought by the T&P after 1925.

The company owned and operated several sand and gravel pits in the State of Texas, and one at Greer, Louisiana. The latter was served by a connection with the Rock Island at Turkey Creek by means of the company-owned 2.2 mile long Evangeline Railway. All of its secondhand power was identified with the firm's name spelled out on the tender; the exceptions being Ten-Wheeler No. 217 and Consolidation No. 407 that were lettered for the abbreviated short line itself and, in comparison with pit operations elsewhere, were maintained in a manner befitting a first class carrier. — *A. E. Brown, dec., L. Saillard Collection*

Sold in 1946 to the Gifford-Hill & Company's Evangeline Railway, former T&P D-5 Ten-Wheeler No. 217 retains its original number, but lacks any other identification, shortly after the sale. Its ancestry is overwhelmingly obvious, however.

Below: Five years later, No. 217 serves as a forlorn example of the eventual fate of most secondhand steamers sold to sand and gravel pit operators. Little, if any, major shopping was performed. Older engines were stripped of usable parts to keep newer arrivals in service. No. 217 shows the effect of this practice in April 1951, down to the lack of drive wheel rims. Ironically, its bell and headlight are still intact. The day of the souvenir hunter had not yet arrived. — *A. E. Brown, dec., L. Saillard Collection*

Mineola, Texas, midway between Texarkana and Fort Worth, was the first engine and crew change point for freight trains west of Texarkana. Through trains seldom occupied its six-track arrow-straight holding yards for very long. I-1-dr Texas type No. 663 is headed for the main line and west on July 4, 1951, with 78 "MT" reefers and mixed tonnage. — *R. S. Plummer, Sr., dec.*

FREIGHT POWER
...Impressive

Modern steam freight power on the Texas and Pacific meant one of three wheel arrangements — 2-8-2, 2-10-2 or 2-10-4. The number was deceiving, though, for T&P regularly dispatched its Ten-Wheelers and Pacific types on locals and redball freights alike, especially in Louisiana and east Texas. West Texas, with westbound ruling grades varying from 1.26 to 1.4 percent, was strictly 2-10-4 country. Until the arrival of the I-1 class 2-10-4's, the forty-four class G-1 2-10-2's — built by Baldwin and Alco between 1916 and 1919 — dragged the tonnage over the west Texas' hills. The I-1's and G-1's accounted for 90 percent of the three wheel arrangements; the 2-8-2's totaled just eleven locomotives.

Surprisingly, the eleven class H-2 2-8-2's — shown on the roster herein — were not the first of their type on the T&P. Government benevolence, in the form of the United States Railroad Administration, assigned eleven of the light series 2-8-2's to the T&P in 1918. As coal burners, however, they were less than welcome on an almost exclusively oil burning railroad. Almost before they could turn a wheel on the T&P, they were sent packing to the Rock Island and replaced with eleven oil burners of the same type. These first 2-8-2's were on the T&P roster long enough to be assigned road class H-1, Nos. 550-560. Why their oil burning replacements were numbered in the 800's, instead of continuing the roster numbers at 561, remains inexplicable since prior to their delivery the T&P assigned successive numbers to new locomotives. Numbers 561-599 were left vacant on the roster.

T&P was still receiving its G-1 class 2-10-2's when the new 2-8-2's arrived. The order was split unevenly — for these first heavy haulers on the road — between Baldwin Locomotive and American's Brooks Works. They were an unremarkable engine — typical of their day — built for tonnage hauling not speed. Although the advantage of completely supporting the locomotive firebox on the trailing truck was well-recognized at the time, these T&P 2-10-2's were unique in that their firebox was partially supported over the last pair of drive wheels. In itself, their arrival marked a transition in T&P motive power for they were a major change from the Ten-Wheelers and limited number of 2-8-0's that previously hauled all of the road's freight.

The outgrowth of the 2-10-2 into the famed I-1 class 2-10-4's could be termed as natural progression or it could be considered another noteworthy transition. It was certainly one of great importance for the T&P. What was unusual was the continuation of a ten-coupled engine to meet the rapidly increasing competition of intercity trucks operating over taxpayer supported highways. Horsepower, not tractive effort alone, was the recognized answer. Faced with the same problem some years later, neighbor Cotton Belt opted for dual service 4-8-4's; however, Cotton Belt grades were as nothing compared to the change in elevation of T&P trackage west of Fort Worth, Texas. A locomotive with speed, power, and stamina was a must, if all operating needs and conditions were to be met.

Lima Locomotive Works' Super-Power concept in the form of a 2-8-4 demonstrator, the A-1, was being displayed on various railroads in early 1925. The timing could not have been better. Just four months after the A-1's first test, T&P ordered its first ten 2-10-4's — essentially lengthened A-1's. They arrived on the property in November and December of 1925 as Nos. 600-609 and were the first Super-Power locomotives to go into regular service after construction of the A-1. Between June 1927 and late 1929, Lima would deliver four more orders of these Texas types for a total of 70 engines — the largest single grouping of Lima Super-Power locomotives.

The new locomotives were impressive, both aesthetically and figuratively. Their appearance would become the hallmark for T&P steam power. The most identifying trademark was an Elesco K-54 feedwater heater mounted high on the smokebox front. The resulting heavy-browed look was accentuated by two pilot-mounted cross-compound air compressors behind angular shaped shields. As built, the 2-10-4's had lengthy wood pilots that were too long for the engines to be coupled nose-to-nose — a fact that enginehouse hostlers frequently forgot. After keeping the shop carpenters overly busy replacing the wood spokes, conventional steel strap pilots were installed. Another T&P trademark added to those engines ordered after the first ten — and applied also to these later on — was an ornate capped stack. Lima's trademark in the form of a large, angular sand dome was an identifying feature on all engines. A second and more conventional-shaped sand dome was applied to the last order Nos. 655-669.

Regardless of the 2-10-4's massive front end appearance it was lean and lanky when viewed broadside. A cab height of 15 feet 5-3/4 inches and an engine length of 60 feet 4 inches was by no means insignificant. The 63-inch drivers, generous opening between firebox and Lima's low-profile trailing truck and unbroken rear silhouette of the sloping boiler imparted a false impression of its true size.

In August 1929, before ordering the last of its Texas types, the T&P actually considered an elongated version of the 2-10-4 in the form of a 4-10-6. This proposed engine, a heavier- and higher-drivered 67-inch model, was to have both a trailing- and tender-truck mounted booster engine that together would have exerted 116,000 pounds of tractive effort. It was not built, of course, and T&P's fleet of Texas types finished out at a total of 70 engines. Excepting the Pennsylvania's 125 J-1 class, the I-1's were the largest group of 2-10-4's built.

Unfortunately the new 2-10-4's were so poorly counterbalanced that they were restricted to a speed limit of 45 m.p.h. — a limit not always obeyed. This, together with the continuing need for faster train schedules, resulted in all of the engines receiving new lightweight nickel-steel main and side rods, Baldwin disc main drive wheels, and valve pilots, between 1927 and 1941. The letter "r," following the locomotive classification letter, identified those rebuilt. The work was done by the T&P at its Fort Worth and Marshall, Texas, shops.

In an effort to further improve upon the 2-10-4's and to compete with the new upstart diesel-electric proposed by Electro-Motive as a replacement, ten of the Texas types were chosen at random, in 1947, for rebuilding with one-piece cast steel frames with integral cylinders, Timken roller bearings on all axles, Laird style crossheads, either Baldwin disc or Boxpok driving wheels and Delta trailing trucks. During the rebuilding in July 1948, the T&P had a change of mind and ordered 72 new diesel freight units from EMD. Nine of the Texas types had been rebuilt, the remaining and unused cast-steel engine frame was scrapped. Upgraded Texas type No. 650 made the last revenue freight run on August 25, 1951. With the exception of Nos. 610 and 638 — set aside for display — all were scrapped by May 1953.

T&P STEAM FREIGHT LOCOMOTIVES
1925 - 1953

Class	Wheel Type	Numbers	Builder and Date	Cylinders (Bore x Stroke) (In Inches)	Drive Wheel Diameter (In Inches)	Boiler Pressure Lbs.	Grate Area (Sq. Ft.)	Engine Weight (Lbs.)	Tractive Force (Lbs.)	Remarks
H-2	2-8-2	800-810	BLW 1919	26 x 30	63	200	66.7	292,000	54,700	See notes

(All rebuilt 1939-42 with lightweight rods, disc drivers, multiple bearing crossheads and K-40A Elesco feedwater heaters. No. 800, 801, 803-805, 807-810 received G-1-c 2-10-2 tenders; 4,000 gals., oil, 12,000 gals., water. Nos. 802 and 806 received G-1-b 2-10-2 tenders; 5,000 gals., oil, 15,000 gals. water.)

Class	Wheel Type	Numbers	Builder and Date	Cylinders	Drive Wheel Diameter	Boiler Pressure	Grate Area	Engine Weight	Tractive Force	Remarks
G-1	2-10-2	500-505	BLW 1916	28 x 32	63	200	70	328,500	67,700	All scrapped by 1937
G-1-a	2-10-2	506-513	BLW 1917	28 x 32	63	200	70	328,500	67,700	All scrapped by 1937
G-1-b	2-10-2	514-525	BLW 1919	28 x 32	63	200	70	339,300	67,700	All scrapped by 1949

(All rebuilt 1928-30 with Delta trailing trucks and booster adding 11,800 lbs., T.E., K-40A Elesco feedwater heater and tenders with 5,000 gals., oil, 15,000 gals., water.)

Class	Wheel Type	Numbers	Builder and Date	Cylinders	Drive Wheel Diameter	Boiler Pressure	Grate Area	Engine Weight	Tractive Force	Remarks
G-1-c	2-10-2	526-543	Alco-Brooks 1919	28 x 32	63	200	70	332,000	67,700	All scrapped by 1949

(Nos. 527, 529, 531, 534, 535, 539 sold to National of Mexico Railway in 1941-42)

Class	Wheel Type	Numbers	Builder and Date	Cylinders	Drive Wheel Diameter	Boiler Pressure	Grate Area	Engine Weight	Tractive Force	Remarks
I-1	2-10-4	600-609	Lima 1925	29 x 32	63	255	100	448,000	84,600	See notes
I-1-a	2-10-4	610-624	Lima 1927	29 x 32	63	255	100	448,000	84,600	See notes
I-1-b	2-10-4	625-639	Lima 2-1928	29 x 32	63	255	100	452,000	84,600	See notes
I-1-c	2-10-4	640-654	Lima 6-1928	29 x 32	63	255	100	452,000	84,600	See notes
I-1-d	2-10-4	655-669	Lima 1929	29 x 32	63	255	100	457,000	84,600	See notes

(All engines equipped with trailing truck booster adding 13,300 lbs., tractive force.)
(All dimensions shown are for engines as built. For class designations after rebuildings refer to page 52.)
(With exception of Nos. 610 and 638 all engines scrapped by May 1953.)

The T&P was second only to the Nickel Plate Road in making its USRA design light 2-8-2's appear larger and more impressive than they really were. Pilot deck mounted air compressors, Elesco feed-water heater, and a tender equalling in size those of the 2-10-4's, helped to create an engine of seemingly gigantic proportions. Left- and right-hand views of No. 806 at Alexandria, Louisiana, in 1949, show the effect. — *C. T. Felstead*

No. 54 on the T&P's operating timecard was a scheduled redball freight run of great urgency between Fort Worth, Texas, and New Orleans, Louisiana. With not one but two auxiliary water cars coupled to its tender to insure a minimum of stops, heavy shielded Mikado No. 802 shatters the noon hour quietude of Bunkie, Louisiana, in its thundering determination to reach the Crescent City on time. — *E. Robinson*

Despite its gray-green boiler and cylinder jacketing and the Texas & Pacific lettering on its tender, the obvious parentage of No. 400 — as a former Burlington Route (Fort Worth and Denver) engine — is too apparent to hide. Five years after the last of the T&P's steamers were scrapped the 2-8-2 was purchased, in May 1958, for use in times of high water on the lines east of Shreveport, Louisiana. When not in use, it was stored in the Shreveport engine house and classed as work equipment. It was finally put on display at Marshall, Texas. — *A. E. Brown, dec., C. E. Winters Collection*

A brand new I-1 2-10-4 Texas type, No. 653, is definitely other than an all-black locomotive as it sits outside Lima Locomotive's erecting shops in June 1928. Its boiler and cylinder jacketing, external dry pipe, and booster pipe are painted in the glossy gray-green color that was traditional for T&P steam power. One can only lament the lack of color photography at the time. — *Allen County Historical Society*

The five basic classes of T&P 2-10-4's varied little in appearance and only slightly in dimensions, as built. The second group, class I-1-a, Nos. 610-624, had several changes from the original I-1 engines that were incorporated into all of the classes following. All were minor changes but indicative of the need to better a good thing; boiler pressure was increased from 250 to 255 pounds increasing the original tractive effort of 83,000 pounds to 84,600; an Elesco K-50A feedwater heater replaced the original K-54 model; an American Multiple Throttle replaced the Chambers type. This last change allowed room for the stack to be capped with an ornate flange.

The last of the series, the I-1-d class, incorporated several modifications gained from experience with the earlier built engines. A second, round-shaped, sand dome was added over the firebox and the original dome was moved forward. The three inch drypipe was eliminated from the left side of the boiler. A centrifugal pump mounted ahead of the trailing truck — on the engine's left side — replaced the original Elesco CF-1 feedwater heater pump. More significant, but not so obvious, was the addition of one-piece cast cylinders. Although significant, these changes were small in comparison to those the T&P itself would make between 1937 and 1941. These later changes would see the original five engine classifications expanded to eleven. Beginning in December 1937 all of the 2-10-4's were to be rebuilt with valve pilots, lightweight nickel-steel main and side rods, and disc main drivers, on a first-in, first-out basis, regardless of number. No. 601 was the first engine to be rebuilt and No. 669, the last, in August 1941. All rebuilts were identified with an "r" following the classification letter, e.g., I-1-a became I-1-ar.

Obviously delighted with the performance of the 2-10-4's, T&P shortly after putting them into service, not only contemplated but drew-up plans for a 557,000 pound 4-10-6 type locomotive, in 1929. This proposed monster was to have a 120-square foot grate area and a booster unit on both the locomotive trailing truck and the lead tender

No. 615 — the recipient of lightweight nickel-steel main and side rods, disc main and rear drivers, and Illinois Central-style rear sand dome in the 1937-41 rebuilding — at Fort Worth, Texas, in 1948. — C. T. Felstead

truck. The road, however, decided to stay with a tried and true machine, ordering an additional 15 2-10-4's, class I-1-d, Nos. 655-669, in August 1929, bringing the roster total to 70 — a number exceeded only by the Pennsylvania Railroad's 125 J-1 class.

In a last ditch attempt to stem the tide of dieselization, then T&P Superintendent of Motive Power, L. E. Dix, convinced W. G. Vollmer, President of the road, that a fully equipped roller-bearing I-1 could do anything a diesel could do. Accordingly, ten one-piece cast-steel frames were received from the General Steel Castings Company, and a like number of I class engines were chosen at random for inclusion of these new frames and cylinders, plus Timken roller bearings throughout. New Laird-type roller bearing crossheads, Baldwin disc or Boxpok driving wheels, and Delta trailing trucks were also applied during this rebuilding. These rebuilts were classified as I-2 with No. 644 being the first engine completed in November 1947.

Nos. 650, 616, 657, 664, 608, 625, 649, and 636 were also upgraded with all work completed in June 1949. This left the tenth frame as yet unused. Even with these extensive improvements, a single 2-10-4 equaled only two EMD F-7 diesel units, in tonnage ratings. It was a valiant and expensive attempt, but it failed. The unused frame was scrapped while the I-1 and I-2 classes followed suit in rapid succession. The upgraded No. 650 made the last revenue run of a T&P 2-10-4 from Mineola to Texarkana on August 12, 1951, and was the last of the series to be scrapped at Marshall, Texas, on May 26, 1953.

Clean track ballast and Texas' daisies add contrast to a newly arrived I-1 No. 609 making its debut run with revenue tonnage west of Fort Worth, Texas, in 1925. — *Allen County Historical Society*

I-1 No. 606 at Fort Worth, Texas, 1948.

Tall stack, and Laird-type roller bearing crossheads on No. 618, versus a shorter stack, added sand dome, disc wheels, and original Alligator-style crossheads on No. 620 — both I-1-ar class of 1927 — reflect the random, and sometimes erratic, improvements to T&P's 2-10-4's. — *C. T. Felstead*

No. 662 is near the crest of a typical Texas' undulation and the effect of the slack running out on 80 plus loaded boxcars is beginning to show as the 2-10-4 digs in on the upgrade near Atlanta, Texas, in this 1938 scene. — *H. Stirton Collection*

Paying heed to slow orders during track renewal work, 2-10-4 No.
640 eases by the umbrella sheds of the Dallas Union Terminal, in
June 1950, with a long eastbound freight. — *R. S. Plummer, Sr.,
dec.*

Opposite left: No. 635 at Fort
Worth, Texas, in 1948. — *F. E.
Ardrey, Jr., Collection*

X-585.

Head-on views of 2-10-4 No. 610, new, at the builders in 1925, and 52 years later in service on a Southern Railway steam excursion at Lexington, Kentucky, in 1977. No. 610 — undoubtedly the most famous of all T&P steam locomotives — was presented to the Southwestern Exposition and Fat Stock Show at Fort Worth, Texas, on January 27, 1951, and placed on display near the Will Rogers Memorial Coliseum. It was rehabilitated in 1976 — by the 610 Historical Foundation — to power the nation's bicentennial train while on tour in Texas and thereafter leased to the Southern Railway, in 1977, to power that road's famous excursion trains across the southeastern United States. — *New view, K. M. Kohls; E. P. Herzog, Jr.*

In view of I-1-a No. 610 being the only remaining number of the T&P's famed 2-10-4's, it was a fortunate coincidence that Lima's photographer chose the engine, in 1925, for a series of close-up views in and under its cab. — *K. M. Kohls Collection*

Displaying Southern Railway emblems on its air pump shields and the omnipresent gold eagle — symbol of the Southern's motive power heritage — atop its headlight, No. 610 smokes up the countryside on an excursion trip between Huntingburg, Indiana, and Louisville, Kentucky, in June 1978. Even though pulling an auxiliary water car and twenty-four loaded passenger cars, No. 610 made light work of the Indiana hills but yet delighted lineside photographers with Mt. Etna-like outpourings of oil smoke exhaust at every turn of her drivers. — *E. P. Herzog, Jr.*

Making its last revenue freight run, 2-10-4 No. 638 charges out of the Mineola, Texas, yards, in mid-1949, with 57 tank cars loaded with Texas crude oil bound for eastern refineries. A few months later, on December 22, 1949, wrapped in a garland of red ribbon, No. 638 was presented to the State Fair at Dallas, Texas, for permanent exhibition. A short five years later, in 1955, the once powerful machine had become so unsightly from pillage and damage at the hands of thieves and vandals that it was scrapped. — *R. S. Plummer, Sr., dec.*

P-1-r Pacific No. 700 is all T&P, and all business, roaring down the main line south of Bunkie, Louisiana, with New Orleans bound train No. 24 on April 23, 1943. — *E. Robinson*

PASSENGER POWER
...Elegant

With only three wheel arrangements comprising the heavy freight power of the Texas and Pacific from 1925 until the end of steam operations, it is not surprising that the carrier's primary passenger locomotive roster, during those same years, was represented by only two wheel arrangements — the 4-6-2 Pacific and 4-8-2 Mountain types.

In actuality, T&P listed two 4-4-0 Eight-Wheelers, thirty-eight 4-6-0 Ten-Wheelers, and two 4-4-2 Atlantic types as passenger power in its 1926 roster. While the Ten-Wheelers continued to share passenger train duties with the newer Pacific and Mountain types, the 4-4-0's were scrapped in late 1926. Due to poor performance, Atlantic types Nos. 339 and 340 were written off shortly after their construction in 1906 by the T&P and, although numbers 341-349 were reserved for future such engines, their type was not repeated. Nos. 339 and 340 were scrapped in 1928. Little photographic evidence remains attesting to their having existed.

The total number of Pacific types on the T&P roster was 22 — a small number in comparison to those operated by many another class one rail carrier. Locomotive numbers ran consecutively from 700 to 721 and were divided into three separate classes, P-1, P-1-a and P-1-b, determined by date of construction. The seven P-1 class engines, Nos. 700-706, built by Baldwin, were completed in April 1919. They were delivered as Nos. 600-606 but were renumbered shortly before the second group of P-1-a's, Nos. 707-713, arrived from Alco's Brooks Works later the same year. Since consecutive numbering of its motive power had been its practice, the reason for this change in numbering sequence is unknown. It is as though the coming of the 2-10-4's was foretold. Four years later, in 1923, the P-1-b class engines, Nos. 714-721, were received from Alco's Richmond Works.

Basic dimensions and looks of the 4-6-2's, as built, were relatively the same. Such simplicity would not last, however. Rebuildings and improvements in ensuing years — especially during the locomotive modernization program begun in 1938 — resulted in a complexity of subclasses and appearances. Engines that received roller bearings on all axles had an "r" added to their class designation. Variations could be found in tender size and locomotive frontal features. Tender capacities ranged from original four-wheel truck styles of 9,000 gallon capacity to six-wheel trucks supporting a 15,000 gallon tank. These larger tenders — usually from scrapped G-1 class 2-10-2's — angular air pump shields and Elesco feedwater heaters combined to present a machine of impressive proportions and power for a 4-6-2 type. Add to this the T&P's adopted color scheme for its passenger power of a gray-green painted boiler and cylinder jacketing, polished nickel-steel cylinder head covers and flanged stack, glossy black domes, and red-painted T&P emblems on the pilot deck shields and the result was visually superb.

Pacific No. 700 makes for a double feature as it leaves Shreveport, Louisiana, in the early morning with train No. 21, *The Louisiana Limited,* and rolls over a street viaduct advertising its very consist. The train came overnight from New Orleans and will connect with No. 1, *The Sunshine Special,* at Marshall, Texas, where its sleepers will be added to *The Special's* consist for forwarding to Dallas, El Paso, and Los Angeles as advertised. — *E. Robinson*

Pacific No. 701 roars out of the dark and into the dawn at 6:45 A.M. at Shreveport, Louisiana, with train No. 21 from New Orleans headed for connections at Marshall, Texas, in 1942. — *E. Robinson*

P-1-b No. 721 at Fort Worth, Texas, in 1948, is about as covered with piping and accessories as an engine could be! The result is almost brutish at first glance. — *C. T. Felstead Collection*

Friend and fellow fireman, E. A. Prince, has P-1-a Pacific No. 712 pouring out a Vesuvius display of smoke right on location as the flanged-stack engine roars past photographer Ed Robinson with train No. 27 near Reisor, Louisiana, on a winter's day in 1950.

Below: Blue and silver Pacific No. 719 leans into a banked curve near Reisor, Louisiana, at seventy miles an hour with New Orleans bound No. 28 in mid-1950. — *E. Robinson*

Looking pretty much as built — with original small capacity tender and wood spoke pilot — Pacific No. 721 hurries eleven cars of No. 26, *The Louisiana Limited,* out of Shreveport, Louisiana, in 1937. — *H. Stirton Collection*

The ten heavyweights of train No. 27 are going like the proverbial bat out of Hades across the wintry Louisiana landscape behind a roaring, smoke-belching 4-6-2. No. 702's 73-inch drivers are no hindrance in hitting the eighty mile an hour mark on the flat straightaway near Reisor on February 6, 1943. — *E. Robinson*

All, save one, of the T&P's passenger runs from Texarkana to Fort Worth, Texas, went over the main line via Marshall and Dallas. The lone exception was train No. 31 routed via Sherman, Paris, and Denton. A makes-all-stops daylight schedule, No. 31 averaged 31 miles an hour on the seven and one-half hour, 245 mile run. Jack rabbit starts and seventy miles an hour running were necessary to maintain a schedule calling for eighteen stops and a possible twelve flag stops. No. 31 is pictured here charging out of Paris on the advertised behind P-1-b No. 715 in the fall of 1941. — *R. S. Plummer, Sr., dec.*

Following the inauguration of the blue and gray diesel-powered *Texas Eagle* on August 15, 1948, T&P repainted a number of its P-1 class 4-6-2's in a matching color scheme and assigned them to Nos. 27 and 28, a New Orleans train that connected with the streamliner at Marshall, Texas. The blue and silver of No. 710, however fleeting, is in stark contrast to the lush Louisiana greenery surrounding the Bayou Pierre trestle south of Shreveport. — *E. Robinson*

Pacific No. 710 has just emerged from the Marshall, Texas, shops, in July 1949, resplendent in a coat of *Eagle* blue paint set off by a silvered smokebox and a gray and silver striped tender. — *R. S. Plummer, Sr., dec.*

For those T&P Pacific types painted in the blue and gray *Eagle* paint scheme, the change was often more than cosmetic. A larger tender, slanted cab front, disc drivers, and an extended turret cover are obvious differences between Nos. 700, 701, and 704. — *No. 700, C. T. Felstead Collection; No. 701, C. E. Winters Collection*

Its nickel steel stack flange all the more brilliant from the reflection of the silver painted smokebox, blue painted Pacific No. 712 roars across a ballasted-deck wood trestle south of Shreveport, Louisiana, with six cars of train No. 27 in the summer of 1950. — *E. Robinson*

With only one green coach to break up its otherwise all blue and gray consist, P-1-r No. 706 sweeps across a long curving trestle east of Janesville, Texas, in August 1950, with No. 28. The gloved hand of engineer Walter Simpson has the big Pacific holding at seventy per. — *E. Robinson*

Pacific types Nos. 704 and 706 had the dubious distinction — out of all such engines painted in *Eagle* blue and gray — to be fitted with running board skirts that carried forward to the smokebox the two-foot-high gray and silver trimmed band on the tender. The riveted steel panels — with their obvious homemade appearance — did little to enhance the engine. No. 704 rides the turntable at Marshall, Texas, immediately after receiving its adornment in July 1949, while No. 709 displays its wings at Dallas' Union Terminal in 1950. — *R. S. Plummer, Sr., dec.*

P-1-a Pacific No. 700 is a mass of smoke, steam, and churning drivers as it roars away from a stop at Bunkie, Louisiana, with New Orleans bound train No. 24 at 8 A.M. on a June day in 1949. — E. Robinson

With the towering profile of the T&P's own turreted office building — added to Fort Worth's skyline by T&P's President Lancaster in 1931 — in the background, Pacific No. 702 wheels the eleven cars of No. 27, *The Louisiana Limited*, away from the station platforms at the building's base and across the Santa Fe main line at the east end of the station complex. — *R. S. Plummer, Sr., dec.*

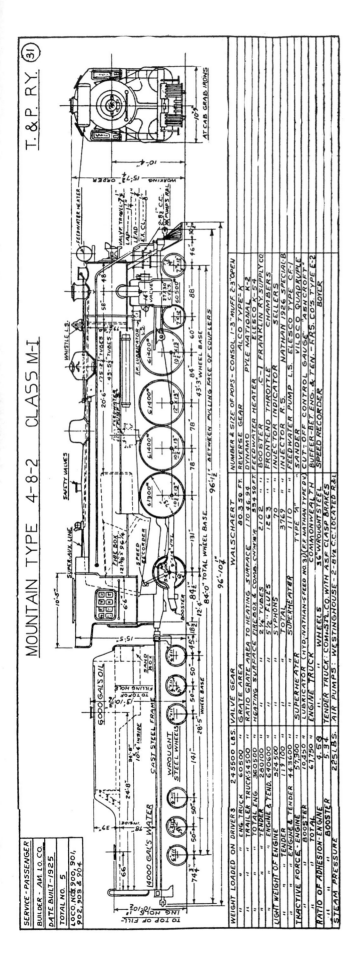

Opposite left: As built M-1 No. 902 makes a station stop at Marshall, Texas, in February 1930. The almost five year old engine displays original wood pilot, front stairs, external dry pipe, and a tender carrying 5,000 gallons of oil and 12,000 gallons of water. Shoppings — in 1938-40 — to replace the original spoke drivers with Boxpok centers on the main and fourth drivers also resulted in larger tender bodies with a capacity of 6,000 gallons of oil and 14,000 gallons of water. — *Railroad Museum of Pennsylvania (PHMC)*

Its nickel steel cylinder heads reflecting the late afternoon sun, M-1 No. 900 roars over a rural grade crossing and cattle guard as it accelerates the twelve cars of No. 7, *The Southerner,* west from Marshall, Texas, in the summer of 1944. No. 7 was the secondary passenger train over the T&P, originating in St. Louis, Missouri, on the Missouri Pacific and running all the way to El Paso, Texas, with connections to Los Angeles via the Southern Pacific. — *E. Robinson*

Emerging from what was then — in 1935 — considered a man-made canyon of brick and steel, M-2 Mountain type No. 907 works up speed leaving Dallas, Texas, with No. 15, *The Texan.* — *A. E. Brown, dec., L. Saillard Collection*

To anyone familiar with a Boston & Maine 2-8-4 or a Central Vermont 2-8-0, it is hard to imagine that the same Coffin feedwater heater that gave those engines their beetle-browed look was also applied to this T&P 4-8-2. Enclosed in the front portion of its smokebox, No. 906 hides its unit well. At Fort Worth, in 1947. — *C. T. Felstead Collection*

Unlike the Coffin feedwater heaters as applied to the M-2 Mountain types, Elesco type heaters could not easily be hidden within the smokebox but were instead a very visible part of the locomotive. M-1 No. 903 carries its Elesco unit well while waiting to forward the West Texas section of *The Sunshine Special* from Fort Worth to El Paso, Texas, in 1947. — *R. Collins*

The Texas Ranger in action! T&P's overnight run, No. 6, from El Paso, Texas — with more head-end revenue equipment than rider cars, from as far west as the California coast — tops the heavy grade east of Fort Worth behind the straining rods and staccato exhaust of Mountain type No. 905. At Marshall, Texas, its consist will be split up and sent east and north on other scheduled runs.

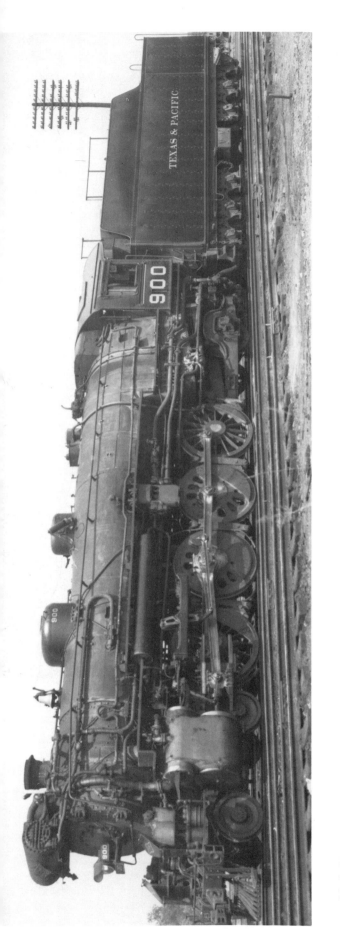

M-1's Nos. 900 and 901 show their form at Fort Worth, in 1947. — No. 900, F. E. Ardrey, Jr., Collection; No. 901, C. T. Felstead

84

Within sight of the Dallas Union Station, M-2 No. 908 thunders across the Trinity River Bridge on the west side of the city with the sixteen heavyweight coaches, diner, and sleeping cars of No. 8, *The Westerner,* on the last lap of its 863 mile run across the State of Texas. The well-polished 4-8-2 is one of three M-2 engines displaying gold pin striping on its sand dome, cab, and tender sides. It will run through to Texarkana where the major portion of its consist will be turned over to the Missouri Pacific for forwarding to St. Louis. — *R. S. Plummer, Sr., dec.*

M-1 No. 903 announces its arrival into Texarkana with a billowing plume of oil exhaust, with northbound train No. 208 from Longview, Texas. — *R. S. Plummer, Sr., dec.*

Photographer Roger S. Plummer, Sr., captured more than he bargained for when recording Kansas City Southern's redball freight No. 77 headed south out of Texarkana behind four red, yellow, and black F units, in 1949. T&P's M-1 No. 901, working up to speed with *The Southerner* on the parallel main line, roared into view at the same time to provide this action-filled scene of steam and diesel in its short-lived race for dominance.

Aside from their original wooden pilots being replaced with those of steel strap construction, no major modifications were made to the M1 and M2 class engines other than attempts at better wheel balancing. Boxpok center drive wheels replaced original spoke drivers on No. 903, in 1938, and No. 904, in 1940, with the remainder of the two classes having their main and third set of drivers replaced with Boxpok during the 1940's. No. 904 shows the effect at Marshall, Texas, in 1944. — *E. Robinson*

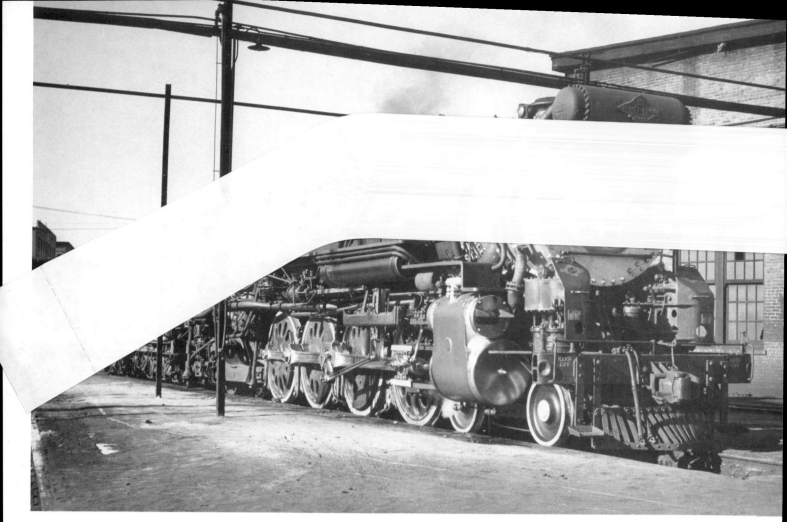

Five of the M-1 and M-2 class 4-8-2's, Nos. 900, 902, 904, 907, and 908, were painted in the matching blue and gray paint scheme of the diesel-powered *Eagle* stream-liners. Opinions vary as to whether or not it was an improvement over the gray-green and black that had been a long-standing hallmark of T&P steam power. There was little disagreement, though, on its being one of the more colorful and unusual paint schemes applied to a steam locomotive. The nearly all-blue attire of the loco-

motive itself was neither unusual nor distasteful, but the treatment of the tender with a plain gray center band outlined with silver stripes was a bit on the garish side.

No. 902, sitting on the Texarkana ready tracks, in 1949, is a veritable rainbow of color in an area given to the blacks and grays associated with steam operations. — *R. S. Plummer, Sr., dec.*

The hogger of M-1 No. 900 has the blue and gray painted Mountain type stepping smartly away from the Texarkana station platforms in June 1949 with the twelve cars of No. 7, *The Southerner,* on its makes-all-stops west of Fort Worth schedule, that will see it in El Paso at 6:30 P.M. the following evening. — *R. S. Plummer, Sr., dec.*

Opposite left: Awaiting assignment on the garden tracks of the Texarkana enginehouse, in 1946, M-2 No. 908 displays a short-lived and limited use of gold pin striping on its sand dome and decorative filigree on its tender sides. Nos. 901 and 905 were the only other M class 4-8-2's to be thus decorated.

Baldwin's photograph of C-2 No. 480 reveals the abundance of piping and flexible joints required to carry the engine's exhaust steam to the auxiliary engine attached to the front tender truck. Although a proven success at its assigned task, its available tractive force was entirely dependent on the amount of fuel and water in the tender.

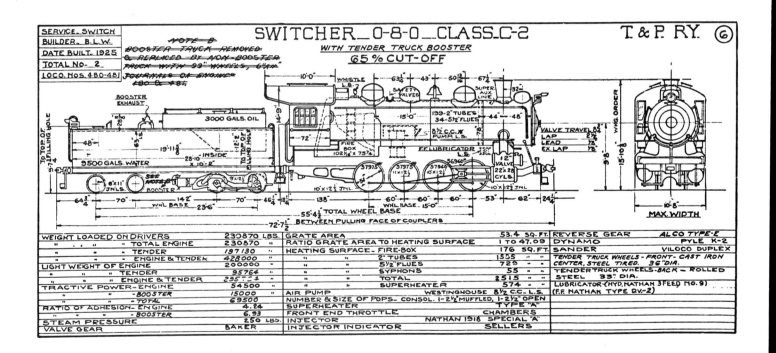

YARD POWER
...Elementary

As late as August 1923 the T&P locomotive roster listed six 2-6-0 Mogul types, designated class C-1, as yard service engines. It also listed fifty-seven 0-6-0 types. By January 1926 all of the Moguls and one 0-6-0 had left the freight yards for the scrap yards and ten new 0-8-0's, class C-2, had taken their place. An extreme change in motive power, to say the least.

T&P yard power, like its road power, remained conservative in size and numbers throughout the first quarter of the century. The 0-6-0 was the dominant yard power until the arrival of the first 0-8-0's in 1925. As late as January 1923 Alco's Cooke Works delivered eight class B-8-a 0-6-0 types. Heaviest and most powerful of the type were the fourteen USRA design B-8 engines delivered by Alco's Pittsburgh Works in March 1919. An uncommonly small roster of yard power, for a carrier the size of the T&P, but understandable, considering the amount of older Mogul and Ten-Wheelers assigned to all but the larger freight terminals.

Advent of the I class 2-10-4's, in 1925 — and the additional freight traffic their speed and power was expected to generate — brought about the need for larger and better yard power. While Lima built all of the 2-10-4's, Baldwin received the orders for all fifteen of the new 0-8-0 switch engines beginning with the C-2 class, Nos. 480-489, in 1925, and ending with the C-2-a class, Nos. 490-494, in 1927. Regardless of front-end throttles and capped stacks, engine size, weight, and tractive effort was comparable to that of the government designed 0-8-0's of the United States Railroad Administration. What did set four of the new engines apart, however, was the application of a Franklin auxiliary locomotive booster to the front tender trucks that added 15,000 pounds of tractive effort. Two of the C-2 class, Nos. 480 and 481, and two of the C-2-a class, Nos. 490 and 491, were recipients of this device. Its application was predicated upon their doubling as yard engines at Baird, Texas, and as pushing power for westbound freights climbing the 1.3 percent grade to the *Llano Estacado* ("Staked Plains") that form the High Plains of West Texas, west of Baird. Instances of 0-8-0 switch engines assisting heavy freight trains into motion at many major rail terminals was commonplace, but the specific design and planned usage of yard power for helper service was rare. Displaced 2-8-2's and 2-10-2's occasionally filled in as helper engines on Baird Hill but the booster equipped 0-8-0's held sway until the later years of steam when they could be found more frequently working the hump at Fort Worth's Lancaster yard.

If anything set the T&P's B-7 class of 0-6-0's apart from their contemporaries it was their impression of height as compared to the rail-hugging tendencies of the USRA sponsored B-8 class. Slope-back tenders were another trademark of the class. Regardless of appearance, the B-7's 57-inch drive wheels and light engine weight made them the lesser in tractive power. No. 456, at Jury, Texas, in 1950, shows little change from No. 450, at Baldwin, in 1916. — *No. 456, C. T. Felstead Collection*

92

T&P STEAM SWITCHERS IN SERVICE AFTER 1925

Class	Wheel Type	Numbers	Builder and Date	Cylinders (Bore x Stroke) (In Inches)	Drive Wheel Diameter (In Inches)	Boiler Pressure Lbs.	Grate Area (Sq. Ft.)	Engine Weight (Lbs.)	Tractive Force (Lbs.)	Remarks
B-5	0-6-0	3, 8, 10, 15	T&P 1907	17 x 24	52	150	14.5	78,000	17,300	See note
B-5	0-6-0	22, 23, 25	T&P 1902	17 x 24	52	150	14.5	78,000	17,300	See note
B-5	0-6-0	27	T&P 1903	17 x 24	52	150	14.5	78,000	17,300	See note
B-5	0-6-0	41, 46	T&P 1905	17 x 24	52	150	14.5	78,000	17,300	See note
B-5	0-6-0	113-115	T&P 1901	17 x 24	52	150	14.5	78,000	17,300	See note
B-5	0-6-0	127-134	T&P 1898-1900	17 x 24	52	150	14.5	78,000	17,300	See note
B-5	0-6-0	140, 169	T&P 1907	17 x 24	52	150	14.5	78,000	17,300	See note

(Nos. 127-134 rebuilt from original Rogers built Missouri Pacific 4-4-0 types by T&P. No. 15 sold to Gifford-Hill Co., 1915. All others scrapped between 1-1926 and 9-1936.)

Class	Wheel Type	Numbers	Builder and Date	Cylinders	Drive Wheel Diameter	Boiler Pressure Lbs.	Grate Area	Engine Weight	Tractive Force	Remarks
B-6	0-6-0	317-323	Cooke 1902	20 x 26	52	175	31.5	130,000	30,400	See note

(Nos. 318, 319, 320-322 sold to Gifford-Hill Co. No. 317 scrapped 12-1948. No. 323 sold to S. W. Materials Co., 11-1949)

| B-7 | 0-6-0 | 450-456 | BLW 1916 | 21 x 28 | 57 | 185 | 44 | 158,700 | 39,100 | See note |

(No. 456 sold to Gifford-Hill Co., 11-1948. All others scrapped by 12-1948.)

| B-8 | 0-6-0 | 457-470 | Alco-Pitts 1919 | 21 x 28 | 51 | 190 | 33 | 165,000 | 39,100 | See note |

(No. 458 to Arkansas & Louisiana Missouri Ry., 1-50, No. 463 to Gifford-Hill Co., 10-51. All others scrapped by 1949.)

| B-8-a | 0-6-0 | 471-478 | Alco-Cooke 1923 | 21 x 28 | 51 | 190 | 33 | 160,000 | 39,100 | See note |

(Nos. 472 and 478 to Louisiana Eastern Ry., all others scrapped by 1949)

| C-2 | 0-8-0 | 480, 481 | BLW 1925 | 22 x 28 | 51 | 250 | 53.4 | 230,870 | 54,000 | See note |

(Engines equipped with tender booster adding 15,000 lbs., tractive force.)

| C-2 | 0-8-0 | 482-489 | BLW 1925 | 22 x 28 | 51 | 250 | 53.4 | 228,530 | 54,500 | |
| C-2-a | 0-8-0 | 490, 491 | BLW 1927 | 22 x 28 | 51 | 250 | 53.4 | 232,800 | 54,500 | See note |

(Engines equipped with tender booster adding 15,000 lbs., tractive force.)

| C-2-a | 0-8-0 | 492-494 | BLW 1927 | 22 x 28 | 51 | 250 | 53.4 | 230,500 | 54,500 | |

93

USRA original 0-6-0 No. 470, a class B-8, still trails its government-designed tender with high bunker sides at Fort Worth, Texas, in 1935. In comparison, copy No. 478, a B-8-a, also at Fort Worth, but in 1948, displays a cut-down version of the same style tender. The eight B-8-a engines, built in 1923, were duplicates of the previous 1919-built USRA engines. — *C. T. Felstead Collection*

Judging from the firmly held broom emerging from the front cab door of No. 460, at Fort Worth, Texas, in 1947, the engine is about to have its running boards swept clean. — *F. E. Ardrey, Jr., Collection*

The longest living examples of the T&P's B-6 class 0-6-0 switchers were Nos. 320 and 323. Both engines ended their days shuffling cars in small division point yards in Louisiana. No. 323 was in service the longest, surviving until January 1949. The fiesty little veteran rides the turntable at Addis, Louisiana, on December 12, 1947. — *R. J. Foster, dec., C. T. Felstead Collection*

Front-end throttles were a feature of both T&P and Missouri Pacific 0-8-0's. No. 488 at Shreveport, Louisiana, in 1948. — *C. T. Felstead*

C-2-a No. 490 is typical of the appearance attributed to the T&P 0-8-0's, e.g., flanged stack, front-end throttle, tender booster, and oil burning. While all of the C-2-a class were delivered with flanged stacks, none of the C-2's, Nos. 480-489, were fitted with the decoration, and only Nos. 490 and 491 of the C-2-a class were equipped with a tender booster. The first two numbers of the C-2 class were also the only numbers equipped with tender boosters. One of these was equipped, for a short period of time, with boosters on both front and rear trucks for use on the long grade approach to the Huey P. Long Bridge at New Orleans, Louisiana, but the 0-8-0's steam supply was insufficient for any tangible increase in tractive effort and the rear unit was removed. — *H. K. Vollrath Collection*

Both Nos. 493 and 494 work the Fort Worth yards in 1948.

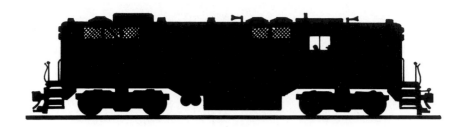

DIESEL ELECTRICS
...EMD Minus One

If ever there was a class one railroad that was loyal to one particular diesel-electric locomotive manufacturer it was the Texas and Pacific. With one exception, its completely dieselized roster of April 1952 was comprised of all Electro-Motive built units. In contrast to its parent Missouri Pacific Lines that indulged in Alco, Baldwin and, to a minor extent, Fairbanks-Morse units, T&P remained a loyal EMD customer.

T&P effected full dieselization with a total of 222 units, comprised of 46 switch engines, 40 road switchers, 18 E-7A and E-8A passenger units, and 118 F-7 A&B freight units. Standardization also existed within its own ranks in that no FT, F-3 or F-9 freight units were purchased. All of these units were purchased between 1946 and 1960, with the bulk of the roster acquired in the four-year period from 1949 to 1952.

The lone exception to the carrier's all EMD roster was an American Locomotive built RS-2, No. 1100, delivered in January 1949. Its intrusion into the ranks of F-7's and GP-7's was short-lived; first being sold to the T&P-MP Terminal in New Orleans, Louisiana, in March 1952, then to the MP as its No. 958, thence to the Alton and Southern Railroad as its second No. 33 and, finally, to the Precision Engineering Company in partial trade for an ex-D&RGW F-7A No. 849.

Inspection of the tabulated roster will reveal a novel and practical method used by the T&P in the numbering of its diesel power. With the exception of the GP series road switchers, all units were numbered to correspond with their horsepower rating, e.g., all of the 2000-2011 series E-7A's were rated at 2000 horsepower. A minor variation occurred with the E-8A's, however, in their not being assigned numbers to match their 2250 horsepower rating. Also, even though in compliance with this numbering sequence, the 800 horsepower SW-8 switchers could not start with the even 800 figure as the 800-810 series 2-8-2 steam locomotives were still very much in service at the time the switchers were delivered in 1951.

The choice of EMD as the standard builder for its diesel fleet appears to have been an easy one; the choice of a standard paint scheme for these same locomotives was another matter. While all of the E and F units arrived in the blue and gray of parent Missouri Pacific, and remained so until 1960, colors chosen for the switchers and road switchers varied from solid black for the SW-8's and NW-2's to a gaudy combination of black and, as termed by the railroad, "Swamp Holly Orange," for the SW-7 and SW-9 switchers and the GP-7 road switchers. The first group of GP-9's, Nos. 1131-1136, were delivered in 1957 in the orange and black scheme but were repainted in 1960 to match the paint scheme of the second order of GP-9's, Nos. 1137-1144, that arrived in MoPac blue and gray but in a different color arrangement. Management had considered a duplication of the MoPac color scheme but chose instead to use gray as the dominant color with an arrangement of blue stripes that had to be a high-maintenance expense. Oddly enough, none of the GP-7's were repainted in the gray and blue scheme.

Four of the F-7A units, Nos. 1500, 1501, 1581, 1582, and their accompanying B units, Nos. 1531B-1534B, were regeared for possible passenger service between 1952 and 1958 and, with the exception of No. 1501, repainted in the same configuration as the E units. T&P's first low hood, or chopped-nose, units were five GP-18's, Nos. 1145-1149, delivered in May 1960. These were the last units to display the carrier's custom paint scheme. Full merger with the parent MoPac in 1962 resulted not only in all units being renumbered into the MoPac system but repainted in the overall dark blue referred to as *Eagle* blue — more appropriately termed Downing B. Jenks' blue for the President of the MoPac who designated its use on all locomotives.

Regardless of their sameness of color, freight and passenger units on the T&P in the covered wagon era of diesel power were readily identifiable by their color schemes. The MoPac inspired *Eagle* symbol on the front of all passenger power also revealed the locomotive's assignment. E-8A No. 2017 and F-7A No. 1522, idling nose-to-nose on the Texarkana engine leads, in 1952, are apt evidence of this identifying difference. — *R. S. Plummer, Sr., dec.*

TEXAS & PACIFIC RAILWAY
DIESEL-ELECTRIC LOCOMOTIVES

All locomotives built by General Motors,
Electro-Motive Division except for RS-2
No. 1100 built by Alco-GE.

NUMBERS	HORSEPOWER	MODEL	DATE BUILT	M.P. ASSIGNED NUMBERS OF 1962	
811-818	800	SW-8	1952	8000-8007	
1000-1001	1000	NW-2	1946	Retained T&P Nos.	
1002-1008	1000	NW-2	1947	Retained T&P Nos.	
1009-1014	1000	NW-2	1948	Retained T&P Nos.	
1015-1019	1000	NW-2	1949	Retained T&P Nos.	
1020-1023	1200	SW-7	1950	1215-1218	
1024-1036	1200	SW-9	1951	1219-1231	
1100	1500	RS-2	1949	See note	
1110-1116	1500	GP-7	1950	110-116	
1117-1124	1500	GP-7	1951	117-124	
1125-1130	1500	GP-7	1952	125-130	
1131-1136	1750	GP-9	1957	386-392	DB
1137-1144	1750	GP-9	1959	393-399	DB
1145-1149	1800	GP-18	1960	500-504	DB
1500-1519	1500	F-7A	1949	850-869	DB
1520-1536	1500	F-7A	1950	870-886	DB
1537-1580	1500	F-7A	1951	887-930	DB
1581-1582	1500	F-7A	1952	931-932	DB
1500B-1515B	1500	F-7B	1949	850B-865B	DB
1516B-1517B	1500	F-7B	1950	866B-867B	DB
1518B-1530B	1500	F-7B	1951	868B-880B	DB
1531B-1534B	1500	F-7B	1952	881B-884B	DB
2000-2007	2000	E-7A	1947	1-8	SG
2008-2009	2000	E-7A	1949	9-10	SG
2010-2017	2250	E-8A	1951	30-37	SG
600-613	2500	GP-35	1964	MP assigned Nos.	
640-649	2500	GP-35	1965	MP assigned Nos.	
1280-1299	1200	SW-1200	1966	MP assigned Nos.	

Notes: RS-2 No. 1100 became No. 23 of T&P-MP Terminal Railroad of New Orleans in May 1952. Renumbered 958 in 1962. Became Alton & Southern's second No. 33 in 1968.

Nos. 1500, 1501, 1581, 1582, 1531B-1534B re-geared and modified for passenger service during period 12-1952 to 6-1958.

DB—Dynamic Brake
SG—Steam Generator

GP-7's Nos. 1111 and 1124, in Swamp Holly Orange and black, idle in the Texas' sun at Fort Worth and Denton, in 1951 and 1952, respectively. Both units lost their first digit in the MoPac renumbering of 1962. — *C. M. Mizell, Jr.*

GP-7 No. 1130 in blue and gray at Shreveport, Louisiana, in October 1960. — *H. K. Vollrath Collection*

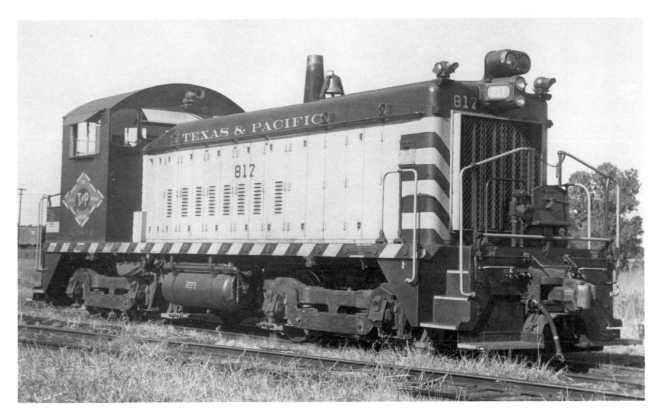

Its front heavy with lighting apparatus, SW-8 No. 817 idles in the moderate-sized yards at Grand Saline, Texas, in May 1955. — C. M. Mizell, Jr.

No. 1005 is one of seven EMD NW-2 switchers built in 1947 that retained its original number after the T&P's merger with the MoPac. The pumpkin colored unit idles in the Dallas, Texas, yards in 1959. — C. M. Mizell, Jr.

Swamp Holly Orange and blue and gray team up in a three unit combination of diesel power at Mineola, Texas, in 1951. — *R. S. Plummer, Sr., dec.*

GP-7 No. 1119 is in *Eagle* blue and gray paint at New Orleans, Louisiana, in 1955. — *R. H. Carlson Collection*

Above: F-7A diesel No. 1581, at New Orleans, Louisiana, in 1954, is one of four such A units, Nos. 1500, 1501, 1581, and 1582, along with four accompanying B units, Nos. 1531-1534, that were regeared and repainted for passenger service between December 1952 and June 1958. — *R. H. Carlson Collection*

A pioneer in T&P dieselization, 1949 EMD built F-7A, No. 1506, leads a westbound freight out of the Texarkana yards in August 1951. — *R. S. Plummer, Sr., dec.*

A trio of F-7A and B units, headed by No. 1540, are leading one empty boxcar and 87 refrigerator cars of Rio Grande Valley produce north toward Texarkana in June 1951. — *R. S. Plummer, Sr., dec.*

F-7A No. 1500 was one of the four units regeared for passenger service in 1952. It was normally coupled to an E-7A or E-8A unit and used on Fort Worth to New Orleans trains where the full 4,000 plus horsepower of two E units was not necessary. It is shown here, painted in the *Eagle* color scheme, at Dallas, Texas, in 1960. — *C. M. Mizell, Jr.*

With all but three of its thirteen car consist made up of head-end revenue cars, T&P's No. 15, *The Texan,* clatters over the Belt Junction crossing near Dallas, Texas, in June 1952, on its way west behind a regeared F-7A No. 1581 and E-8A No. 2013. — *R. S. Plummer, Sr., dec.*

Another of the regeared F-7A's, No. 1582, is serving as a B unit between two E-8A's on a heavy El Paso bound passenger train at Dallas, Texas, in 1960. — *C. M. Mizell, Jr.*

The Streamliners — E-7A No. 2001 and E-8A No. 2010, new at EMD in 1947 and 1951, respectively. — *EMD Photos, R. L. Hundman Collection*

Protected by a pair of the Southern Pacific's distinctive lower quadrant semaphore signals, a pair of EMD E-7A diesel units, headed by No. 2006, glides onto the El Paso, Texas, station trackage with No. 7, *The Southerner*, to complete almost 24 hours of travel across the width of Texas. — *E. Robinson*

Below: E-8A No. 2010 and E-7A No. 2000 are teamed up to power No. 8 east out of Dallas, Texas, in September 1959. — *C. M. Mizell, Jr.*

The normal blue and gray consist of train No. 26 on the New Orleans, Louisiana, to Marshall, Texas, haul is broken sharply by the purple and silver of an Atlantic Coast Line baggage-express car as E-8A No. 2015 speeds over well-ballasted rail near Shreveport in 1962.

No. 27, on the reverse haul, behind E-8A No. 2016, exhibits the same inconsistency due to an all stainless-steel Southern Pacific coach near the rear of its otherwise matched consist. — *A. E. Brown, dec., F. E. Ardrey, Jr., Collection*

On May 31, 1969 — one day before government sponsored Amtrak assumed the nation's passenger train operations — Missouri Pacific's E-8A's Nos. 35 and 30, formerly T&P's Nos. 2015 and 2010, wait to move the last scheduled passenger run out of the Dallas Union Terminal. — *C. M. Mizell, Jr.*

The rare and the elusive. T&P's one and only Alco product, RS-2 No. 1100, in its as-delivered paint scheme of overall black with gold striping and a red, black, gold, and silver emblem, at the Fort Worth passenger station in 1949. Unsuccessful in its first assignment at the Lancaster hump yard it was repainted in Swamp Holly Orange and black and transferred to Texarkana where it worked the passenger station until sold to the T&P-MP Terminal Railroad of New Orleans for their No. 23 in May 1952. — *Tom Stamey Collection*

Looking more like a freight haul than a scheduled passenger run, the 15 express reefers, boxcars, mail-storage cars, RPO cars, coaches, and Pullmans of No. 7, *The Southerner*, head west from Texarkana, Texas, behind a well-polished blue and gray E-7A No. 2002, in October 1951. — *R. S. Plummer, Sr., dec.*

Sharing adjacent stalls as did their steam predecessors T&P's F-7A No. 1570 and GP-7 No. 1127 snuggle up close to a solitary MoPac Alco FA unit No. 320 in the Texarkana engine house in 1958. — *R. S. Plummer, Sr., dec.*

With the last "All Aboard," called out by the conductor twelve cars to the rear, the engineer of a matched pair of E-7A's, Nos. 2000 and 2001, unleashes their combined 4,000 horsepower to move train No. 7, *The Southerner,* away from the Texarkana station platform and west to Dallas, Fort Worth and El Paso. The matched pair of MoPac Alco PA units, headed by No. 8027, that brought the train the full distance from St. Louis, Missouri, idles on the left. — *R. S. Plummer, Sr., dec.*

F-7A No. 1537 and its trailing counterpart, sitting on the ready tracks at Mineola, Texas, in 1958, are as spick-and-span as the day they were delivered in 1951. — *R. S. Plummer, Sr., dec.*

A wealth of early diesel power abounds in this 1957 scene at Texarkana, Texas. Alco, EMD, and Baldwin road units of the Missouri Pacific surround the engine house in the background while a five-unit lash-up of T&P F-7A's and a single orange painted GP-7 growl into motion with a westbound freight. — *R. S. Plummer, Sr., dec.*

A well-scrubbed E-8A No. 2014 and its E-7A mate are placed on the ready track at the Texarkana station by an orange and black NW-2 switcher to await the arrival of a southbound passenger run from the MoPac. — *R. S. Plummer, Sr., dec.*

E-7A's, Nos. 2008 and 2009, accelerate after a station stop at Mineola, Texas, with train No. 21, a makes-all-stops run between Texarkana and Dallas, Texas, in the summer of 1959. — *R. S. Plummer, Sr., dec.*

114

Above: Train No. 208, from Houston, Texas, to St. Louis, Missouri, operating via Palestine and Longview, Texas, on the Mo-Pac, and from Longview to Texarkana, Texas, on the T&P, is in the twilight of its years as its abbreviated six-car consist is brought into the Texarkana yards by E 7A No. 2004 and an E-8A, in 1957. — *R. S. Plummer, Sr., dec.*

A pair of matched F-7A's, Nos. 1518 and 1519, are pulling out of a passing siding west of Marshall, Texas, in July 1956 with a westbound freight after letting an eastbound counterpart pass on the main line. — *R. S. Plummer, Sr., dec.*

T&P did not indulge in Alco's famed PA series diesel passenger locomotives as did parent MoPac, but its EMD E-7A and E-8A units rubbed noses frequently with these northern neighbors at their joint Texarkana engine terminal. T&P's original E-7A, No. 2000, its blue paint heavily faded by the Texas' sun, idles next to a more shiny MoPac PA, No. 8027, in 1958. — *R. S. Plummer, Sr., dec.*

As typified by highway caution signs across the nation, it is an established fact that yellow and black present the most contrast of any two colors. T&P's choice of orange and black for its early yard and road switcher diesel units could not have been measurably far behind in contrast. Although chosen to match the color of the flower of the Swamp Holly plant that abounds in the lush bayou country of lower Texas and Louisiana, the effect was more synonymous with the heat waves of west Texas in midsummer. GP-7 No. 1130 shows the color best at Fort Worth, Texas, in 1955, while No. 111, also at Fort Worth, shows the effects of the Texas' sun. No. 111, the former No. 1111, has had the first digit of its number deleted in keeping with newly assigned MoPac numbers of 1962, and very shortly will have its faded orange replaced by the cool blue of its new owner. — *No. 111, C. A. Duckworth Collection; No. 1130, R. S. Plummer, Sr., dec.*

GP-9 No. 1137 was the forerunner of the blue and gray paint scheme for the T&P's general purpose units. Delivered by EMD in the color scheme shown here at Fort Worth in 1959, it was a radical change from the orange and black of the six duplicate units, Nos. 1131-1136, preceding No. 1137's arrival in 1957. These earlier built units were repainted to match No. 1137 in 1960. Oddly enough none of the GP-7 units was repainted in the interim scheme but remained orange and black until covered entirely in MoPac Jenks' blue. — *C. A. Duckworth Collection.*

NW-2 1008 brightens the Fort Worth, Texas, yards, *circa* 1955. — *C. A. Duckworth Collection*

Right: A pair of E-7A's, headed by No. 2007, roll off the main line into the Texarkana station with the eight cars of northbound train No. 8, *The Southerner*, in June 1958. — *R. S. Plummer, Sr., dec.*

Four units of MoPac early EMD freight power are displayed in full length against a background of the Texarkana station and its umbrella sheds. T&P's singularly company-built caboose No. 2500, with its exceptionally high cupola, is as the lower left, while a T&P NW-2 works the freight leads in this 1958 scene. — *R. S. Plummer Sr., dec.*

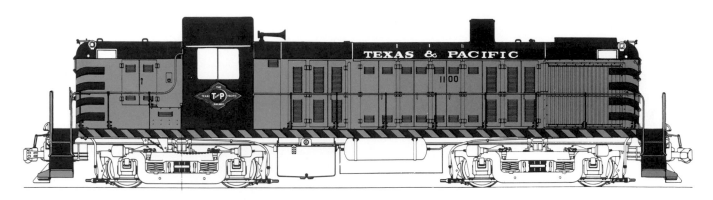

Above: An unduly prolonged search for a color photograph of the elusive No. 1100 in its Swamp Holly Orange paint scheme was unsuccessful and, in lieu thereof, a mechanical drawing of this Texas' loner in its most colorful garb is introduced here. — *Artwork by the author based on T&P stencilling diagrams*

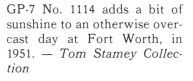

GP-7 No. 1114 adds a bit of sunshine to an otherwise overcast day at Fort Worth, in 1951. — *Tom Stamey Collection*

Unlike a tiger, the T&P could, and did, change its stripes. GP-7 No. 1125 and GP-9 No. 1132 show the before and after at Fort Worth, Texas, in the mid-1950's. Both engines were delivered in No. 1125's orange and black livery but No. 1132 was repainted in blue and gray in 1959. — *C. A. Duckworth Collection*

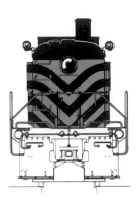

F-7A No. 1582 displays its newly applied passenger unit paint scheme on the Fort Worth turntable, in 1958. — *Tom Stamey Collection*

Flowing sinuously over the arid West Texas' desert, an eastbound one hundred car T&P freight train is an awesome sight as it is led by five F-7 diesel units around a relatively obscure horseshoe curve at Torcer — twelve miles west of Sierra Blanca — on Southern Pacific trackage. Within sight of the twin peaks of Sierra Blanca, the curve provided a gain of 35 feet in elevation, in just under one mile, and was the highest point of operation for the T&P. The ability of modern diesel power to singlehandedly surmount steep grades — where steam power required helpers and lengthier ascents provided by such curves — obviated the need for such geographic landmarks. Thus the curve was eliminated by the SP during a track relocation project in 1960.

The majority of the train's consist is loaded PFE refrigerator cars that were turned over to the T&P at El Paso, under a long standing traffic arrangement between the two carriers. — *Tom Stamey Collection*

119

Rebirth, albeit short-lived, of an I-1. No. 610 shows the world what the eyes of Texas feasted upon for almost three decades. Temporarily lettered for its lessor, the big 2-10-4 shows its muscle on the Southern Railway's Huntingburg, Indiana, to Louisville, Kentucky, district, in 1978.

The T&P's line west from Big Spring to El Paso, Texas, was fully dieselized by 1950, but 2-10-4's and diesel power alike remained in service east to Fort Worth. With four F-7 units hauling more tonnage than an I-1, fewer freight trains were sent west than arrived from Fort Worth, resulting in a recurring surplus of steam power on hand at Big Spring. Doubleheading of I-1's or with diesel power on eastbound trains thus became commonplace until the next order of F-7's arrived in 1951.

I-1-ar No. 623 and four units of diesel power wait at the east end of the Big Spring yards for No. 2, the eastbound *Sunshine Special,* to pass behind E-7A No. 2004, before following it out onto the main line with a heavy tonnage drag. — *F. Springer, Tom Stamey Collection*

Above: T&P's gateway at Texarkana was, indeed, a busy place, as exemplified by this 1949 view of the passenger, freight, and engine servicing area. Yard switchers are busy working both the passenger station tracks and the freight yard; a 2-10-4 waits for a chance to head west with tonnage, and both steam and diesel power occupy the roundhouse leads. — *R. S. Plummer, Sr., dec.*

Below: In the days of steam operations the outside "garden" tracks of the Texarkana enginehouse were alive with the sight and sound of a score of T&P and MoPac locomotives being serviced and attended to. There wasn't a diesel locomotive in sight on this June day in 1948. — *R. S. Plummer, Sr., dec.*

TEXARKANA
...T&P Gateway

In the lexicon of southwestern railroading, Texarkana, Texas, was one with the legendary Ogden, Utah, of Central Pacific-Union Pacific fame. Just as the diamond stacker crews of Collis P. Huntington and Grenville M. Dodge exchanged their trains of California-bound travelers for return loads of produce, silver, and silk, so also did the crews of the iron horses of the pioneer Cairo & Fulton — predecessor of the Iron Mountain-Missouri Pacific — exchange the goods of the East for the cattle, cotton, and wheat of Texas with the fledgling Texas and Pacific at Texarkana, Texas.

Until the merger of the T&P with the parent Missouri Pacific system in 1976, Texarkana remained the major interchange point between the two carriers. When the first T&P Eight-Wheeler chugged into Texarkana on December 13, 1873, it had to wait two months for the Cairo & Fulton to cross the Red River for the link-up with the East. A true link-up was not accomplished for another six years, however. From its beginning in St. Louis, Missouri, in 1952, the predecessor Pacific Railroad had established as standard a rail spacing of five feet. The St. Louis, Iron Mountain & Southern's predecessor, the Cairo & Fulton, had been built to the same five foot gauge. The T&P, however, had been built to the adopted Eastern standard of four feet, eight and one-half inches. Due to this difference of gauges, transfer of freight and passengers at Texarkana became more than a matter of a switching movement or a change of motive power. Each item of rolling stock had to be placed under a "Nutter Car Hoist" and raised sufficiently to allow the wide gauge trucks of the C&F's, or Iron Mountain's, equipment to be removed and replaced with the "narrow gauge" trucks of the T&P, or, in the case of northbound trains, a reverse procedure. The device was crude by today's engineering standards but, with a generous supply of manual labor, it did the job. The unit was put into operation on May 18, 1874, with through sleeping cars from St. Louis to Houston being the first to have their trucks exchanged. It is doubtful if any passengers slept through the exchange.

By 1876 some 6,918 freight cars had been run through the car hoist and, with this figure increasing daily, either additional hoists or a change of track gauge was eminent. Fortunately, both the Missouri Pacific and the Iron Mountain had decided that the latter was sorely needed. In a record-breaking project completed in 19½ hours, the Iron Mountain changed its gauge to that of the T&P, in 1879, and the "Nutter" hoist was moved elsewhere. Through service between St. Louis, Missouri, and all of Texas through Texarkana was now a reality.

Although the T&P and MP long shared a common yard stretching from Texas into Arkansas, each maintained its own engine terminal at Texarkana. Quite appropriately the T&P's terminal was at the west end of the yard while the MoPac's was at the east end in Arkansas. The latter's enginehouse was a frame, short-length holdover from the Iron Mountain's years, with a turntable length that could accommodate nothing longer than a 2-8-2 or a 4-6-2 locomotive. T&P, on the other hand, found it necessary to lengthen its turntable and enlarge its enginehouse, in 1925, in order to accept the newly arrived 2-10-4 Texas types. Although at the time larger power was not contemplated by the MoPac, a decision, in 1937, to make the new T&P engine facility a shared operation was agreed upon and the practice continued well after dieselization. Adjacent to the Texarkana station platforms and readily visible from the nearby Broad Street or "Texas Viaduct" overpass, the outside engine service tracks were a constant source of enjoyment and a gathering place for the local rail buffs.

The station itself was a fine vantage point from which to observe the Texarkana gateway in action. The building was a large masonry structure, built in 1938, that replaced an earlier structure dating back to the Iron Mountain years. Not overly large when compared to most large city terminals, its six through tracks were, nonetheless, a near-continuous scene of frenzied but organized activity as the sleepers, diners, and mail cars of the jointly operated *Sunshine Special, Texan, Hot Springs Special, The Southerner, The Ozarker,* and the once opulent *City of Mexico* paused there briefly for servicing.

An unusual situation was that of the station building being located in both Texas and Arkansas, with the state line running midway through the building. This state line also bisected the roundhouse stall trackage resulting in the enginehouse being located in the State of Arkansas and the turntable in the State of Texas!

The locomotive terminal, not large by major rail carrier standards, was the most interesting aspect of the joint Texarkana facility. During steam operations, Elesco-browed T&P 2-10-4's vied with the more conventional-faced MoPac 2-8-2's while the always all-black MoPac passenger power played second fiddle to the green and blue boilers of the T&P's same wheel arrangements. T&P's 2-10-4's were the largest power to use the enginehouse until the arrival of the MoPac's 2201-15 class 4-8-4's in 1951. Bumped by new diesel power from their original assignments on the divisions radiating from St. Louis, a number of these engines were transferred to Little Rock-Texarkana runs and, though the I-1's of the T&P were no small machine, these biggies of the MoPac dominated all when present. Their excessive length became all the more evident when the enginehouse force attempted to turn the first arrival and smashed the rear tender steps against a concrete retaining wall on one side of the turntable pit.

Advent of diesel power left the facilities relatively unchanged, with the most visual contrast, again, being the colorful orange and black T&P road-switchers vying with the more conservative blue and gray of the MoPac and T&P's own F and E units. With the completion of the MoPac-T&P merger in 1976, Amtrak operations and run-through freight operations resulted in the engine terminal being relegated to a mere servicing track for yard switchers.

Texarkana's turn-of-the-century railroad station was a rambling brick structure with dirt platforms and little protection from the elements.

Texarkana's second, and last station was this yellow brick structure built at a cost of two million dollars in 1938.

The rather unusual situation of the Arkansas-Texas state line splitting the City of Texarkana and its railroad station down the middle was graphically displayed in this widely circulated postcard of the 1930's. The centerline of the street ending at the station's front entrance is the boundary line between the two states.

125

In the heyday of its operation, the platforms of the Texarkana station were seldom vacant of baggage carts heavy with mail and express. Blue painted M-2 No. 908 waits patiently alongside the cart-congested platforms before heading west with No. 7, *The Southerner*.

T&P 2-10-4's were, without doubt, the largest steam locomotives in regular revenue freight service in the State of Texas, but yet not quite large enough to fill the complete length of the Texarkana turntable. Nonetheless, No. 649, a completely rebuilt I-2-c, leaves little room to spare as it is turned prior to being readied for a run west. — *R. S. Plummer, Sr., dec.*

A wondrous variety of both T&P and MoPac motive power frequented the outside garden tracks of the Texarkana roundhouse in the heyday of steam. T&P's 2-10-4's easily outclassed the usual MoPac 2-8-2's, but the 4-8-2 Mountain types of both roads vied for attention when parked adjacent as T&P's No. 900 and MoPac's No. 5311 are shown here, in 1948. MoPac's power never quite equalled the meticulous maintenance lavished on T&P passenger engines. The 900's tender is a mirror image of its polished rods and cylinder head covers in this scene. The 5311 needs a bath. — *R. S. Plummer, Sr., dec.*

Train watching was a favorite pastime at the Texarkana station with plenty of action to justify the occasion. With a moment of respite at hand, a pair of baggage handlers give I-1 No. 618 a casual once-over as it awaits the high sign to follow the fast disappearing markers of No. 7 west into the Texas' sun.

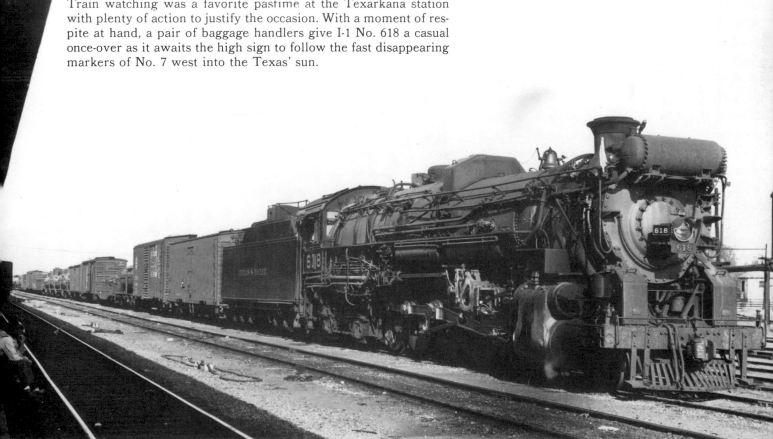

The steam locomotive facilities at Texarkana, Texas, could not boast of a towering coal dock, but did very well with a Roberts and Schaefer coaling device and a like-make cinder disposal system. MoPac's use of coal burning locomotives necessitated such equipment even though T&P locomotives required only fuel oil and water. A sooty-faced MoPac Mikado, No. 1417, and a well-groomed T&P 4-8-2, No. 902, repose alongside their respective needs in 1948. — *R. S. Plummer, Sr., dec.*

E-7A No. 2003 stands idly by, for the moment at least, as blue and gray P-1-b Pacific No. 714 exhausts smartly away from the Texarkana station platforms with the mostly head-end consist of No. 7, *The Southerner*, in 1948. — *R. S. Plummer, Sr., dec.*

Dry sand — and lots of it — was required to put traction under all those drive wheels of a T&P 2-10-4. The hostler's helper balances himself atop the sand dome of I-1-ar No. 612, while filling the angular-shaped reservoir at Texarkana, in 1948. — *R. S. Plummer, Sr., dec.*

The whitewashed walls of the Texarkana roundhouse had not resounded with the sound of steam generators and opening pop valves for some three years when Mr. R. S. Plummer, Sr., recorded a new generation of both T&P and MoPac diesels usurping steam's old hangout; in 1956. Blue and gray freight units of both roads contrast sharply with the Swamp Holly Orange of T&P GP-7 No. 1129 and NW-2 No. 1010.

Left, and opposite: A complete view of all the Texarkana facilities could be had from the Broad Street viaduct spanning the west end of the complex. Although steam power is still in evidence, diesel power dominates, in these 1950 scenes. T&P E-7A No. 2003 departs the passenger station with No. 7, *The Southerner,* for Dallas, Fort Worth and El Paso, followed by the four units of F-7A No. 1518, with a scheduled freight headed in the same direction. MoPac's E-6A No. 7003, idling on the adjacent enginehouse tracks, is considerably off its normal assignment at the head-end of the St. Louis, Missouri, to Denver, Colorado, *Eagle* streamliner. — *R. S. Plummer, Sr., dec.*

Two of the T&P's best in steam share the ready tracks at Texarkana with the forerunner of a host of diesel power yet to come. — *R. S. Plummer, Sr., dec.*

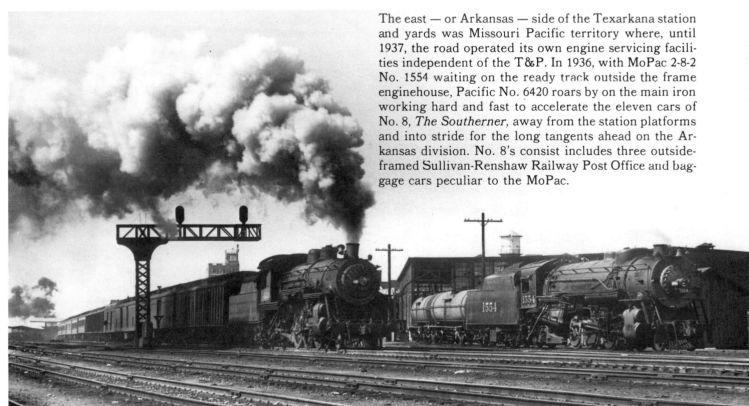

The east — or Arkansas — side of the Texarkana station and yards was Missouri Pacific territory where, until 1937, the road operated its own engine servicing facilities independent of the T&P. In 1936, with MoPac 2-8-2 No. 1554 waiting on the ready track outside the frame enginehouse, Pacific No. 6420 roars by on the main iron working hard and fast to accelerate the eleven cars of No. 8, *The Southerner,* away from the station platforms and into stride for the long tangents ahead on the Arkansas division. No. 8's consist includes three outside-framed Sullivan-Renshaw Railway Post Office and baggage cars peculiar to the MoPac.

131

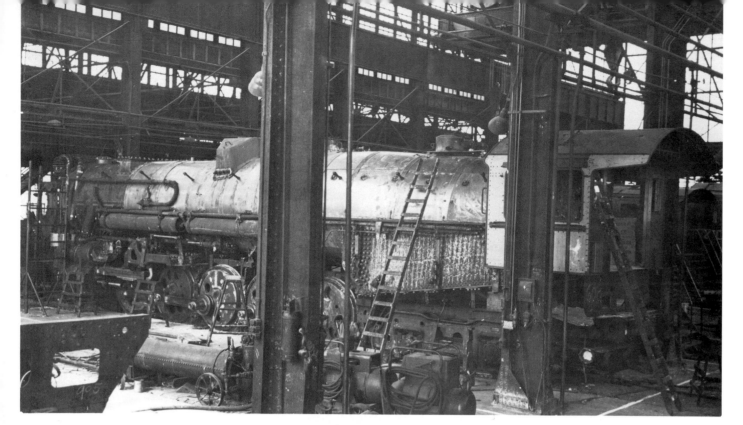

An inside, outside, and overhead view of the T&P's Marshall, Texas, shop complex. Texas type No. 608 is undergoing conversion to an I-2 in June 1949, in the top view, while, in the middle view, a profusion of smaller power awaits shopping or scrapping, in 1940. The bottom aerial view depicts the area shortly after the demise of steam power and conversion of the engine house to a car repair facility in 1958.

T. & P. MISCELLANY

As boxcars roll off the hump into the east end of Fort Worth's Lancaster Yard, I-1-cr No. 645 faces into the western sun and leads a 100-car freight train into the country "Out Where The West Begins." The T&P's relatively flat easterly profile changes drastically west of Fort Worth. Long, heavy grades begin at the 670-foot elevation, at the west end of the yard, and continue intermittently across Texas until the highest point on the railroad, 4,653 feet, is reached — on SP trackage — twelve miles west of Sierra Blanca. The big 2-10-4 has its job cut out for it. — *Tom Stamey Collection*

With two neon lit signs displaying the railroad's name and the corporate emblem on every entrance, the station at Shreveport, Louisiana, is, undeniably, Texas and Pacific property. Its facade is a subtle reflection of the art deco influence of the 1920's.

Below: Dedication day of the new building on May 10, 1940, found disc-drivered, gray-green boilered Pacific No. 712 on display, along with a well-polished coach, diner, and Pullman.

Opposite, top: Ten years later P-1-r Pacific No. 704 departs the modest station trackage, with the eight cars of train No. 27, for Marshall, Texas. —*E. Robinson*

Judging from the station loungers at the T&P's Belcher, Louisiana, depot, train watching on the TS&N branch between Shreveport, Louisiana, and Texarkana, Texas, in 1920, was a less than demanding activity.

Right: The icing dock at Lancaster Yard could simultaneously service forty refrigerator cars.

Below: NW-2 diesel switcher No. 1019 gives a Burlington Route gondola a final nudge to send it over the hump and into the eastbound classification tracks at Lancaster Yard in 1953.

Marshall, Texas — location of the T&P's locomotive and car shops — was an important junction where the lines from New Orleans and Texarkana met and became the main line to Dallas and Fort Worth. The Marshall station was an imposing structure located within the wedge formed by the merging trackage. The depot is little changed in this 1982 photograph, except for the loss of its once-encircling triangle of umbrella sheds as seen behind M-1 Mountain type No. 901 and train No. 2, *The Sunshine Special,* on a late June evening in 1943. — *H. Killam; No. 901, E. Robinson*

Below: Umbrella sheds were yet to be installed in this April 1937 view of M-1 No. 902 slowing to a stop at Marshall with No. 7, *The Southerner.* — *H. K. Vollrath Collection*

Diesel road switchers were not the first T&P property to display the Swamp Holly Orange and black paint scheme. Rural frame depots had long been decorated in the contrasty colors. The Collinsville, Texas, station was decked out for Halloween as far back as 1909, while both Edgewood and Wascom, Texas, displayed the scheme in 1939. — *H. D. Conner, C. A. Duckworth Collection*

Brick station buildings usually remained in their natural state, trimmed with generous amounts of white, such as those at Pecos and Abilene, Texas, in 1976, but the bricks of the Mineola, Texas, station, in 1939, were bright orange accented with black trim. — *Mineola, H. D. Conner, C. A. Duckworth Collection; Others, H. Killam*

139

Bunkie, Louisiana, 169 miles north of New Orleans, was a scheduled stop for all T&P passenger trains, and a favorite haunt of Ed Robinson, photographer at large in this volume. The T&P depot there was mostly functional in appearance, but its generous canopy was more than welcome for waiting train passengers on a hot, muggy Louisiana day. On this summer day in 1941, a couple of early morning station loungers are intent on the arrival of southbound train No. 24 which — per the lighted signal in the distance — is in the block and arrives at Bunkie on the advertised, as promised by both timetable and track circuit.

In stark contrast to the simplicity of Bunkie's brick passenger station, its freight house was colorfully decorated and more indicative of the Cajun Country it served.

Its polished gray-green boiler readily apparent in the late evening sunlight, Ten-Wheeler No. 417 waits obediently at Bunkie station, in August 1938, while the mail, express, and riders of train No. 23 are attended to before hurrying its six cars on toward Marshall, Texas. — *E. Robinson*

140

The T&P actually preceded the Katy Railroad's famous "Sloan" yellow (named for its President Sloan who sanctioned the use of the color) painted 1936 Chrysler Airflow track inspection cars with its own colorful car in the form of this 1927 Lincoln conversion. Wheels, running boards, and fenders were black; and the body was none other than Swamp Holly Orange! It is shown here, still in use at Bunkie, Louisiana, in 1940, with Henry A. Carter, photographer Ed Robinson's cousin, using it for a resting prop.

Union Passenger Station.   EL PASO, Texas.

Roughly halfway between Texarkana, Texas, and Los Angeles, California, El Paso's Union Station is more Southern Pacific than T&P, but it is the official western end of our Texas' carrier. The original building, *circa* 1900, changed little over the years, except for the loss of the peaked roof on its mission style tower in the 1930's.

Reposing naked in the hot Texas' sun, the brick station building at Baird has been stripped of the shady overhang so necessary for creature comfort while awaiting a train. With no riders to worry about in this 1976 view, the operator stays close by a window air conditioner. Baird is at the foot of big, bad Baird Hill — T&P's stepladder to the higher elevations of the *Llano Estacado*, "Staked Plains" of West Texas. — *H. Killam*

Passenger cars pressed into troop train service during World War II were seldom, if ever, air-conditioned and open windows filled with heads and arms were the rule. Three such cars in the consist of No. 24, a Marshall, Texas, to New Orleans, Louisiana, train, are no exception as a P-1-a Pacific on the head-end chants steadily on the long 1.25 percent grade approach to the Huey P. Long Bridge over the Mississippi River in June 1942.

It was the longest — 4.35 miles — steel railway bridge in the world, upriver from New Orleans, completed in December 1935, at a bargain price of fourteen million dollars. Originally used only by the Southern Pacific and the New Orleans Public Belt Railway, the Missouri Pacific and the Texas & Pacific abandoned the use of their river car ferries in favor of the bridge, in 1942. — *E. Robinson*

1928 was a glorious boom year for the T&P, with revenues at an all-time high. Oil traffic peaked at over three million tons for the year. President John Lancaster's newly arrived fleet of 2-10-4 types were moving 3,600 cars a day through the new Lancaster Yard — the first retarder-equipped hump facility in the southwest — at Fort Worth, Texas, while a new locomotive erection shop at the same location was also operative. It seemed only fitting that a suitable monument be erected to all this progress. Thus President Lancaster sanctioned this new combination Fort Worth station and company headquarters — a 12-story stone and brick edifice complete with corner watchtowers and a two-story high winged eagle overlooking it all.

Looking more like a model than an actual building due to the use of a wide angle camera lens — necessary in close city proximity — it is pictured shortly after completion in 1931. — *H. Killam Collection*

T&P was one of the few American railroads to use a boldface, sans-serif stencil style lettering for its identity and reporting marks on freight cars, whereas most other carriers used the thick and thin stroke serif copy commonly referred to as Railroad Roman. Boxcar No. 41200 is one of 250, Nos. 41200-41449, built new at Marshall, Texas, in 1954. — *E. Joseph Collection*

Boxcar No. 82161 is one of 799 cars, Nos. 82000-82798, rebuilt with all-steel superstructures in the Marshall shops during 1950-1959. It was originally a double sheathed wood car, from the series Nos. 50000-50999, built during 1924-25. — *E. Joseph Collection*

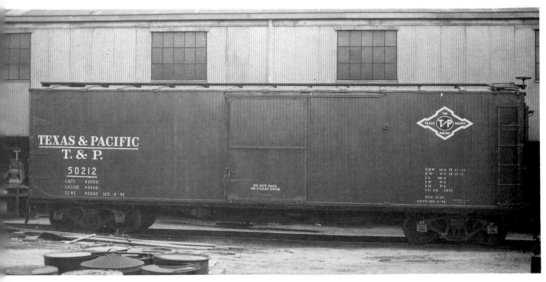

Boxcar No. 50212, photographed outside the Marshall, Texas, car shops in 1946, was typical of the series 50000-50999 rebuilt later, with steel sides and roof, in 1950-59. — *E. Joseph Collection*

Using cars originally built in 1937, T&P's Marshall, Texas, shops refurbished 35 mail storage and express cars, Nos. 1700-1734, in 1954, and painted them in *Eagle* blue, gray, and silver to match existing passenger cars and diesel power. — *E. Joseph Collection*

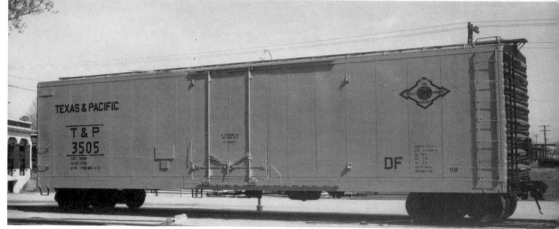

T&P revived its orange and black color scheme for a short time when the Marshall, Texas, shops built 55 DF mechanical refrigerator cars, Nos. 3500-3554, in March 1955. By 1960, the Marshall shops had built a total of 165 of the colorful units. — *E. Joseph Collection*

This 40-foot double sheathed automobile boxcar, No. 50800, one of 2,700 built for the T&P by American Car And Foundry in 1925, was a pioneer in automobile transport. — *AC&F*

145

Above: Gondola cars were the unsung workhorses of a railroad. T&P's No. 19000, first of 401 70-ton gondolas built at the Marshall, Texas, shops between 1951 and 1953. — *E. Joseph Collection*

Right: A 70-ton covered hopper, No. 8600, of series Nos. 8600-8699, built by American Car And Foundry, Berwick, Pennsylvania, in November, 1951.

T&P's 50-foot boxcar, No. 70749, was the forerunner of the modern day double-deck auto-rack car. Hinged doors on one end of the car enabled automobiles to be driven in and chained in place, often in double-deck arrangements. Double side doors made the car usable for other freight, principally lumber, on the return trip. No. 70749 was one of 800 such cars built by American Car And Foundry for the T&P in 1929.

Woodbodied cabooses, Nos. 2323 and 2369, were indicative of the standard "waycar" in use on through T&P freights from the time of their construction in 1928 to their rebuilding, at Marshall, in 1951. Except for the horizontal steel strap bracing on the sides, they were identical to MoPac's standard cabooses built in the same year. — *C. E. Winters Collection*

Just as the 2-10-4 Texas type locomotive was synonymous with the T&P so also was the side door caboose, or "Muley," as it was referred to by T&P crews. The T&P was not the largest owner of stub-ended waycars but did continue their use longer. As late as 1955, 43 remained in service out of a one-time total of 146 prior to 1928.

The lack of end platforms making them dangerous to board while in motion, they were outlawed in states adjacent to Texas for many years prior to a similar Texas' ruling. They could thus be found bringing up the rear of T&P freight drags, well after dieselization.

Nos. 2432 and 2434, still riding on arch-bar trucks in 1950 and 1952, are typical of their appearance for over thirty years. No. 2439, still operational in 1959, has been modernized with Bettendorf-style trucks and a T&P emblem. — *No. 2432, C. E. Winters Collection; No. 2434, W. C. Whittaker; No. 2439, C. A. Duckworth Collection*

In 1949, T&P embarked on a program to rebuild nearly a hundred older woodbodied steel-framed cabooses into all steel units, at its Marshall, Texas, shops. The first, No. 2500, turned out to be a single oddity that was never repeated. Its all-welded construction and overly high cupola set it apart from the remainder of the rebuilts with their riveted construction and lower cupolas. Nos. 2525 and 2526, with their greenhouse cupolas, were more representative of the program's results. A total of 94 cars, Nos. 2500-2593, were outshopped by 1957. — *Nos. 2500, 2526, E. Joseph Collection; No. 2525, Ray S. Curl Collection*

Combination passenger, baggage, and crew caboose, No. 2460, thumping over the Cotton Belt crossing at Texarkana, Texas, in 1950, was one of a pair of such oddities, along with No. 2459, built in 1927 for the T&P. — *C. E. Winters Collection*

Baggage-mail car No. 812 was a stock design car built by American Car And Foundry for several southwestern railroads. T&P had 17 — Nos. 800-816.

Before and after. T&P Railway Post Office car No. 715 has just emerged from the Marshall, Texas, car shops following a face lift that made it compatible with the newer streamlined cars of the *Texas Eagle*. Originally built in 1911 at American Car And Foundry in St. Charles, Missouri — where companion car No. 718 is shown in 1914 — Nos. 715-718 were all cosmetically treated to match the *Eagle* scheme, in 1955. — *No. 715, E. Joseph Collection; No. 718, AC&F*

Under the spreading sycamore tree — a longstanding natural land-mark on the Marshall, Texas, station grounds — stands newly re-painted heavyweight dining car No. 1011, one of nine such cars — Nos. 1011-1022 — that's had its interior and exterior refurbished to add to the harmonious appearance of all the T&P's main line pas-senger consists. — *E. Joseph Collection*

A beautiful example of older heavyweight equipment modernized for continued company use, T&P business car No. 2 has new roller-bearing trucks and tinted windows and is painted in blue and gray to match the *Texas Eagle* streamliner. Sitting at Mar-shall, Texas, in 1957, No. 2 beckons to climb aboard and see the T&P. The road could boast of five near identical cars for official use. — *E. Joseph Collection*

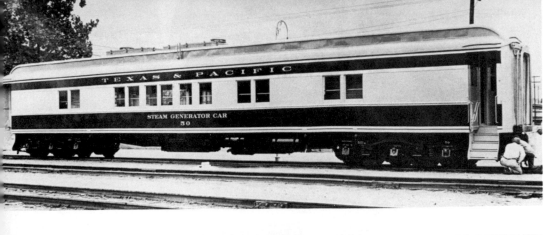

Endeavoring to provide a mobile source of steam for heating and steam-jet air conditioning on passenger cars, the T&P designed and built three steam generator cars, Nos. 50-52, at the Marshall shops in November 1950 and September 1951. With the Korean War straining the railroad's ability to provide diesel passenger locomotives for both regular passenger service and troop train movements on completely dieselized divisions, the cars made it possible to utilize freight diesels not equipped with steam generators. Converted from a steel coach, car No. 50 was equipped with two Vapor-Clarkson 3,500 pound steam generators and was capable of furnishing steam for the continuous operation of a 20-car troop train from Fort Worth to El Paso, 615 miles, before requiring replenishment of its fuel and water supply. — *C. A. Duckworth Collection*

T&P's share of equipment with which to launch the jointly operated MP-T&P *Texas Eagle* streamliners in August 1948, was an even fifty cars. Nineteen were sleeping cars built by Pullman Standard, one a Planetarium dome car from the Budd Company, and a variety of thirty cars built by American Car And Foundry at its St. Charles, Missouri, plant. These consisted of five baggage-mail combines, five baggage-dormitory combines, fourteen coaches, two lounge-grill coaches, one diner, and three diner-lounge cars. In deference to its mostly nighttime schedule and time consuming addition and subtraction of sleeping cars at Little Rock, Arkansas, and Longview, Texas, no observation cars were ordered by either T&P or MoPac.

Nos. 400 and 401 were divided coaches completed in March 1948.

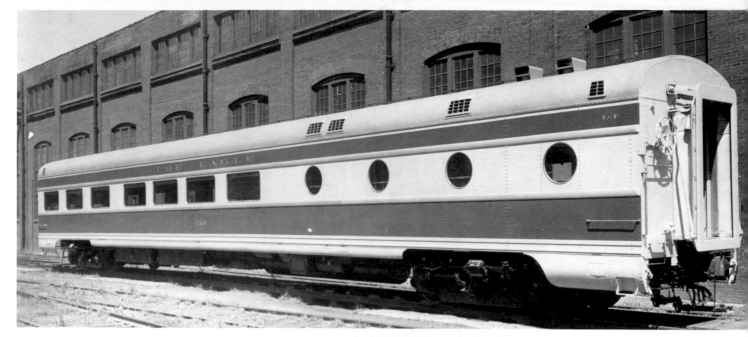

Diner-lounge cars, Nos. 525-527, combined a smoker's lounge and an eight-table dining section, with accompanying kitchen, on *Eagle* connections where a full diner was not warranted. The lounge area and the full lounge and dining area — top and bottom views, respectively — touts smokers with a generous supply of ash trays. — *AC&F*

A long way from the swaybacked, center door "Jim Crow," car typically portrayed plying the rails of a short line through the piney woods or cotton fields of the south, the *Eagle*'s divided grill-coaches continued the separation of white and black patrons. StLB&M car No. 824 is a duplicate of T&P's two such cars, Nos. 480 and 481. — *AC&F*

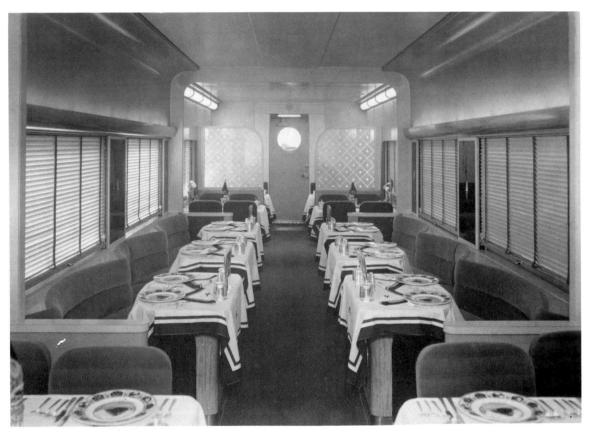

T&P's *Texas Eagle* dining car, No. 500, shown new at the AC&F plant in St. Charles, Missouri, was built with a novel arrangement wherein seating — for six of the 14 tables — was on serpentine shaped settees running lengthwise with the car thereby allowing the diner an unobstructed view through the opposite window. The table settings include the MoPac's colorful dining car china now so highly prized by collectors. These were for display only, with meals being served on plain dinnerware, but could be purchased from the car steward at one dollar each.

The flame of the kerosene-fed torch, carried by No. 700's engineer as he inspected his charge, adds a ghostly appearance to this nighttime exposure at Alexandria, Louisiana, in 1942. The P-1-d Pacific waits to forward train No. 23, *The Texas-Colorado Limited,* west on the first leg of its run between New Orleans, Louisiana, and Marshall, Texas. — *E. Robinson*

The very last T&P steam locomotive in active service was not a magnificent gray-green boilered 2-10-4, but, instead, was a castoff D-5 class 4-6-0 — No. 200 — sold to the Cinclare Central Factory, a sugar refining operation at Cinclare, (Port Allen) Louisiana. Replaced by a secondhand 44-ton diesel switcher at Cinclare, No. 200 was again sold — this time to the Willis Shortline Railroad Co., Inc. for use at a gravel pit operation at Enon, Louisiana, where it served until 1963, and was eventually scrapped there in the late 1970's. — *C. W. Witbeck, L. Saillard Collection*

INDEX

INDEX OF LOCOMOTIVE PHOTOGRAPHS
BY TYPE, NUMBER AND PAGE

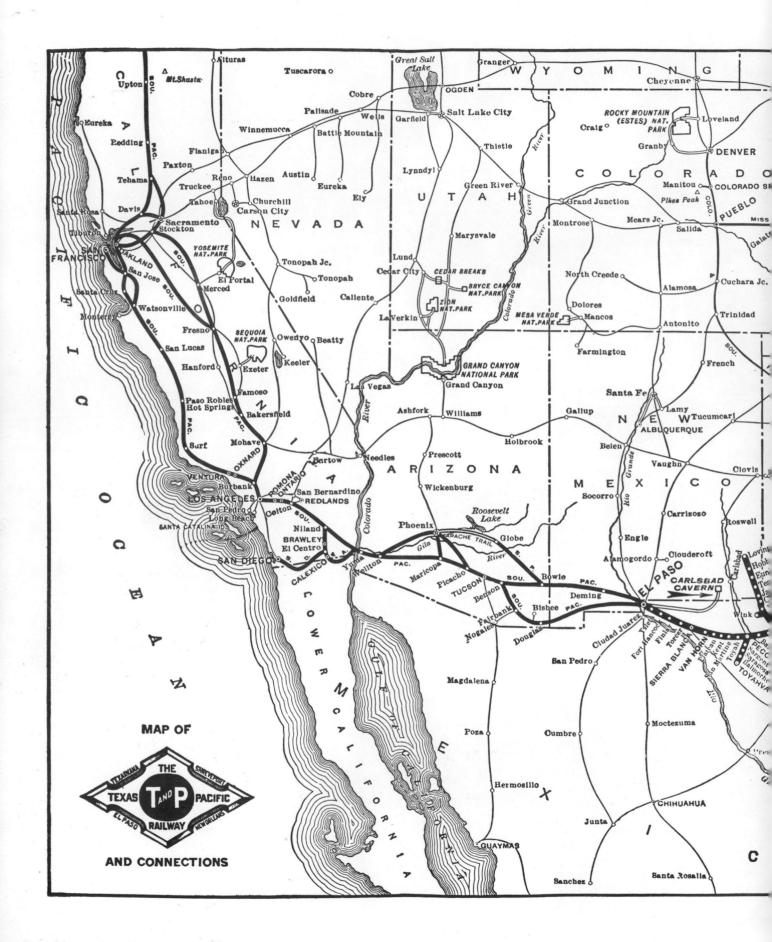

MAP OF

THE TEXAS AND PACIFIC RAILWAY

AND CONNECTIONS